To: J

From:

May the words, thoughts, and scriptures in this book bless your life as you have blessed mine. I am so grateful God crossed our paths and I am so happy we get to spend all of eternity together as Sisters-In-Christ! I Love you to the moon and back.

Bound to the Heart of God

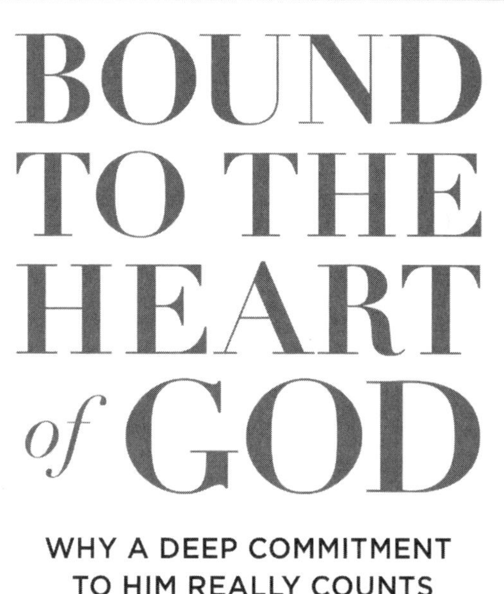
BOUND
TO THE
HEART
of GOD
WHY A DEEP COMMITMENT
TO HIM REALLY COUNTS
A NINETY-DAY JOURNEY

DAN CARROLL

Water of Life
community church

Published by Water of Life
Fontana, California, USA
www.wateroflifecc.org
Printed in the USA

Italics in Scripture quotations are the emphasis of the author.

ISBN-13: 978-0-9913138-9-1

Cover design by Danny Blanton
Interior design by InsideOut CreativeArts

Contents

Preface

All of us know what it's like to be under pressure. Whether it's from our boss, a family member, a medical diagnosis, or on social media, our culture pressures us every day to give in to things like fear, discouragement, or compromise. But we're in good company—many of God's people in the Bible faced the same difficulties we do, or even worse ones. We can learn a lot from them, because they held onto God when things pressed hard against them. In this book we will look specifically at the lives of Nehemiah, David, and Daniel and see how they stood firm when their circumstances and the world around them threatened to blow them up.

This devotional, like my first one (*Into the Heart of God*), is an invitation for you to take a few minutes at the beginning of each day to read and reflect upon a passage of Scripture and what that passage means for you. If we are to become the people God hungers to make us—people who know God, care for others, and are used by God to impact our world—then meeting with God is crucial for each one of us.

I live at the base of the foothills, and I spend most mornings and evenings up the hill communing with God. I am also blessed to spend a lot of time in the Sierra Nevadas each summer hiking and praying. It was during one of these times praying and worshiping on top of Mount Whitney that I took the picture on the front cover. You and I both need times of peaceful quiet with the Lord if we are going to develop the kind of devotion to the Father that Nehemiah, David, and Daniel had. Their relationships with God powerfully affected their circumstances and even changed the world in their days, and our commitment to God can do the same in our day.

The first thirty days of this book focus on preparing ourselves to live abundant lives. God didn't call us to bondage but to freedom and abundance, and some of us need to get hold of this if we want to live boldly for Him. The second thirty days discuss something that none of us likes—difficulties! But the hard things that come our way are under the sovereign control of the Father and often used by Him to test us and shape us for His glory and our good. The good news is, we can walk through trials with steady hearts and strong faith, and when we do, we will become tools in God's hands that He can use to impact others for eternity. The last thirty days talk about deepening our bond with the Father and our commitment to His kingdom. One way this is done is through prayer. It's easy for us to neglect to pray, but that's because we often don't realize how powerful prayer is. Nehemiah, David, and Daniel all prayed boldly and confidently in the midst of some crazy situations, and the results were supernatural. God is looking for people who will prove His power in this world as they reach out to Him in relationship and prayer.

When we decide to follow Jesus, we may not know it, but we are deciding several things that will affect our whole lives: we are deciding to walk with Him and not the world; we are deciding to take the time necessary to cultivate a life-giving relationship with Him; we are deciding to let Him teach us His way, which is far different from our ways; and we are deciding to give up our own lives for the furthering of His kingdom. When we sit down with a devotional book like this one, we are entering into a time of impartation, a time when God can speak life into us. Before you begin each day, ask the Holy Spirit to walk with you and build His destiny into your heart. Please take time to be still, to listen to what He has to say to you. This is the only way we can grow in intimacy with Jesus.

God hungers to satisfy our deepest longings and needs—and the only way that can happen is when we draw near to God and bind our hearts to His. He alone has what each of us needs. Nehemiah, David, Daniel, and many others whose stories we find in the Bible figured this out and lived close to God's heart. None of them were perfect—which ought to encourage us, because none of us are—but they were committed to the Father in a fashion we all ought to long for. I hope the picture of these people who were bound to the heart of God moves you to seek the same kind of relationship with the Father and that He will use you to impact the world.

Days 1–30

Preparing Yourself for Abundant Life

Do you ever ask yourself why you don't thrive more?
Jesus promised us abundant life—
not drudgery or discouragement
but fullness and possibility in the midst of our daily grind.

Day 1

Made to Thrive

The king ordered Asphenaz, his chief of staff, to bring to the palace some of the young men of Judah's royal family and other noble families, who had been brought to Babylon as captives. "Select only strong, healthy, and good-looking young men," he said. . . . They were to be trained for three years, and then they would enter the royal service.

Daniel 1:3–5, NLT

Being taken captive is one of the worst fears a human can face, especially to a foreign land. To become a slave for another's use is almost unimaginable for most of us, yet that is exactly the situation Daniel found himself in as the book of Daniel opens. Yet as we read on, we find that Daniel flourished. Like Joseph, who was also sold into slavery as a teen, Daniel rose to the top of every trial he faced. Undaunted and apparently unshaken, this fifteen-year-old boy from a royal Jewish family somehow not only survived but also thrived.

Do you ever ask yourself why you don't thrive more? Jesus promised us abundant life—not drudgery or discouragement but fullness and possibility in the midst of our daily grind. Daniel figured this out at a very young age, but unfortunately for many of us, bondage is a way of life. No, we are not slaves in a foreign land, but we are in bondage deep within our souls.

Jesus understood this. In Luke 4, when He unrolled the scroll of Isaiah in the temple, He read from a text that ought to cause us to stop and take inventory of our lives: "The Spirit of the LORD is upon me, for he has anointed me to bring Good News to the poor. He has sent me to proclaim that captives will be released, that the blind will see, that the oppressed will be set free, and that the time of the LORD's favor has come" (Luke 4:18–19, NLT).

The word "captive" means literally "one taken into exile," and "oppressed" means to experience severe hardship. Some of us live every day in captivity to severe hardship deep inside our souls. We are stuck—back in grade school, in junior high, in a word that broke us, in a circumstance when someone we trusted tore into us—and we have never gotten free from the pain. This is why Jesus declared that He was called to heal bondage and free captives.

Daniel understood how crucial running to God was for him to survive captivity. We need to do the same. Come to Jesus every time you are weary and heavy in your heart, and He will give you rest. When you start seeing yourself as His and His alone, He will free you from captivity. No one else has bought you; no one else owns you—only Jesus. And He purchased you to set you free. Come to Jesus, and yield your pain to Him today. He has come to heal you.

PRAYER

Father, life is full of bumps and bruises, and I often figure that I am just supposed to live with them. But You have declared freedom over me. I want to believe that You will free me today and heal my scars. Please, Holy Spirit, touch me deep inside, and set me free. Amen.

Day 2

What's in a Name?

The chief of staff renamed them with these Babylonian names: Daniel was called Belteshazzar. Hananiah was called Shadrach. Mishael was called Meshach. Azariah was called Abednego.

Daniel 1:7, NLT

Do you remember when you were in the first grade and had to write your name at the tops of your papers? Our names are often the first words we learn to write because our names are who we are. They shape our identities and sometimes our journeys. The Bible is full of people who had their names changed by God—Abraham, Jacob, Paul. Daniel and his friends received name changes too, but not by God. I am certain that these young men didn't take this lightly.

Hebrews believed that a person's name should reflect his or her nature, so Daniel's parents had named him "God is my judge"; Hananiah's parents had called him "Yahweh is gracious"; Mishael had been named "who is what God is?" (the idea being that there is no god like the God of Israel); and Azariah had been called "Yahweh has helped," or "Yahweh will help." But the Babylonians renamed these four young men after three of their gods. What a shock that must have been to them. We get so much of our identity from our names—and that was the very reason the Babylonians changed these boys' names. They wanted to strip their identities and remake their destinies.

But it didn't work. Daniel and his friends had their identities grounded in something much deeper than their names. Their identities came from their relationships with Yahweh, their God. Our identities should come from the same place: Jesus, our God. He is the One who has purchased our lives. He is the One who has declared us to be His sons or daughters:

> As many as received Him, to them He gave the right to become children of God. (John 1:12)

> Because you are sons, God has sent the Spirit of his Son into our hearts, crying, "Abba! Father." (Gal. 4:6, ESV)

> Even before he made the world, God loved us and chose us in Christ to be holy and without fault in his eyes. God decided in advance to adopt us into his own family by bringing us to himself through Jesus Christ. This is what he wanted to do, and it gave him great pleasure. (Eph. 1:4–5, NLT)

If you know Jesus, your name is not your nature. Jesus is the One who shapes your nature, and He is shaping it at this very moment. He is crafting circumstances to bring you closer to Him and deepen your heart. He is testing you now, today. Can you see His hand moving in your situations? Daniel and his friends recognized God's hand in their lives. In spite of the horrendous situation they were in, they believed that God was bigger than King Nebuchadnezzar and able to move beyond his Babylonian empire. God is still moving in you today.

PRAYER

Father, I need to see Your hand in my journey. Holy Spirit, give me eyes to see and ears to hear what You are saying and doing in my circumstances. I know that You are for me, and I am believing that You will move in me today. Amen.

Day 3

Get on Your Number

Now I was the cupbearer to the king.

Nehemiah 1:11

Where do you find yourself today? You may be a mother or a father, a grandmother or a grandfather, a widow or a divorcee. You may be a single working mother or a professional athlete, a musician or a teacher, an attorney or a contractor. We often find ourselves in places we never expected. Nehemiah surely never imagined when he was growing up as a faithful Jewish boy that he would one day be the most trusted servant of the Babylonian king. We may have gotten into our positions on our own power or even by our own mistakes, or, like Nehemiah, we may have been placed there supernaturally for a divine purpose.

We may find ourselves in a very wrong place today, or we may find ourselves living on our numbers, where God intends us to be. That number, as I like to say, is our place of blessing. Years ago, when I was a PE teacher, I counted students present in class only if they got on their numbers on the blacktop during roll call. If they were on someone else's number, I counted them absent. Our lives are much the same. God has a destiny for us, and we are only blessed and bountiful in this life when we are in it.

The place you find yourself today may be nondescript or even feel meaningless, yet it may be totally God and your destiny. On the other hand, you may feel powerful and important, but the place you have chosen may not have any touch of God on it whatsoever.

Wherever we are, we need to be sure it is where God wants us to be. That is only possible by yielding to Him daily and allowing Him to mark our lives with His hand. When we prayerfully say yes to Jesus every day, we can live with a certainty that many only long for.

If you have been rebellious and have found yielding to God to be difficult, don't panic. He is the One who put the fire in you, but He wants to use it for His glory, just as He did with the apostle Paul. Tell God that you hunger for Him to harness all that is in you for His glory. Say yes to Him today, and say no to all those desires that drive you into despair. Ask the Holy Spirit to work deep in your heart and mind. This simple act of daily surrender can yield so much peace and life that you will be amazed at what He will do in your life.

When we live with the certainty that we have put God first, we can then expect that God will perform miracles in our journeys. He will show up at the most unexpected times when we mark out each day as His.

PRAYER

Holy Spirit, sometimes it is so hard to discern Your will and way. They often seem like a great mystery. But of this I am certain: I hunger to be where You want me to be and to learn all You want me to learn while I am in that place. I want my destiny to be full and rich with the life that only knowing You can bring. Amen.

DAY 4

Friendships Made in Heaven

It came about when he had finished speaking to Saul, that the soul of Jonathan was knit to the soul of David, and Jonathan loved him as himself. . . . Jonathan made a covenant with David because he loved him as himself. Jonathan stripped himself of the robe that was on him and gave it to David, with his armor, including his sword and his bow and his belt.

1 SAMUEL 18:1–4

We all need friendships made in heaven. If you are fortunate enough to have even one friendship like the one David and Jonathan had, you know what I am talking about. Most of my early life was forged in friendships built on brokenness and sin. They were friendships built out of all my friends and I had: emptiness and a worldly view of life. For me those friendships were all about me, and for my friends they were all about them. As long as things were good, we were cool; but when we were short on money or selfish about an issue, it was a nightmare. We turned on each other like a pack of wolves.

This was never the heart of God for people. Some of us begin to grow in Christ, but we never break away from old relationships that wound and tear us down. I distinctly remember the Holy Spirit telling me that it was time for me to move on from these relationships.

But I had to decide that He was right. Finally I did. Had I not done that, I doubt I would have survived and grown in the Lord. I am certain that I wouldn't have thrived, because the only way I have really flourished in the Lord is because godly people have shown me the way.

The love Jonathan and David had for one another was born in the heart of God before it was ever born in their own hearts. God has people He wants in our lives—people who will encourage and build us up and sacrifice to help us, and people whom we will want to sacrifice to help. But we have to get into the places where these people are. Small groups, ministries, outreach trips—these are a few of the places in which the Holy Spirit introduces us to others whose hearts are after Jesus.

If you are lonely today, if you feel abandoned by others, stop and ask the Holy Spirit right now to begin to reshape your heart for His friendships. He will do a deep work in you in this regard if you commit to partnering with Him.

PRAYER

Father, I know that to have life-giving friendships means that I need to be a life-giving person for others. Please work in me. Transform me, Holy Spirit, into a person who is otherly—someone who loves others and desires to push them ahead of myself. Thank You, Lord. Amen.

Day 5

Honoring Others

Jonathan, Saul's son, arose and went to David at Horesh, and encouraged him in God. Thus he said to him, "Do not be afraid, because the hand of Saul my father will not find you, and you will be king over Israel and I will be next to you; and Saul my father knows that also."

1 Samuel 23:16–17

From the first moment God shaped Jonathan's heart, He put in it a deep love for David. Jonathan honored David above himself. This is amazing when we consider that Jonathan was in line to become the next king of Israel and David was a direct threat to that taking place.

Jonathan was older, richer, and far more powerful than David, who was a shepherd boy, yet he understood that his call was to push David ahead of himself. Rather than hungering for position, Jonathan stepped back and honored David. This sort of honoring of others is a lost art in our society. We have all been taught to honor ourselves, not others. Yet Jesus set the example for us when He stepped down from heaven and put us ahead of Himself. Philippians 2:3–7 explains this clearly:

> Don't be selfish; don't try to impress others. Be humble, thinking of others as better than yourselves. Don't look out only for your own interests, but take an interest in others, too. You must have the same attitude that Christ Jesus

> had. Though he was God, he did not think of equality with God as something to cling to. Instead, he gave up his divine privileges; he took the humble position of a slave and was born as a human being. (NLT)

Jonathan's humility and honoring of David allowed God to move on the people of Israel in a way that could have never happened if Jonathan had worried about himself first. Jonathan had a generous spirit. He had a large heart and a desire to move in the will and power of God, even though he had been raised by a father who had a small heart and a selfish spirit. That should give us all hope!

Ask the Lord about your heart in these matters. Do you honor others? Do you ever push them ahead of yourself? Do you have a deep love for them and a desire to see Jesus move in them? Please don't be afraid of stepping aside as the Holy Spirit leads you to honor others ahead of yourself. You can be certain that God will honor you and make a way for you as you trust Him.

PRAYER

Jesus, I know little about honoring others. Will You please teach me how to do this? Holy Spirit, will You give me the grace and courage to honor others ahead of myself? If I am to grow in the heart of Jesus, I must grow in this area of honor. Touch me, and build me in Your image, Father. Thank You! Amen.

Day 6

Humility Like Christ's

Do nothing from selfishness or empty conceit, but with humility of mind regard one another as more important than yourselves; do not merely look out for your own personal interests, but also for the interests of others.

PHILIPPIANS 2:3–4

When Paul wrote his letter to the church in Philippi, he was in prison in Rome, which makes Philippians 2:3–4 an amazing passage. A guy in prison was telling people to put others before themselves, and he himself was doing just that by writing to them and changing the world from his prison cell.

This group of people in the city of Philippi had stood with Paul and supported him both spiritually and financially. But Paul wasn't writing this warm and encouraging letter just to be friendly; no, his purpose was much larger than that. It was about the kingdom of God and changing the world, no matter what his situation looked like. Living out of Jesus' Spirit and moving through the world with a deep love for others was so radical that it had gotten Paul put in jail. Yet he never backed down or lived in fear. Rather, he took the opportunity of sitting in a prison cell to write to God's people about how to love each other, live together well, and honor those around them.

In the midst of instructions on living, Paul jumped into this teaching in chapter 2 on putting others first. It is unlike anything else in the New Testament, giving insight into how Jesus emptied

Himself of His glory as God and took on the likeness of men so we could really know our God. Paul wrote that we should do nothing from selfishness or empty conceit but instead live with humility—a humility that actually puts others before ourselves, like Jesus did. This is what made the early Christians lights in the darkness and hope to the hopeless, and it does the same for us today.

Unselfish and otherly, this thinking puts others first and us second. Without Jesus' presence moving deeply in us and dealing with our selfishness, this can never happen. But this is the heart of the Spirit of God, and it is His job to empower us to love others ahead of ourselves. Only when the Holy Spirit has the reins to our lives can we live with a humility of mind that is not threatening to others but actually welcoming. It embraces people where they are. It gets underneath them and lifts them. It doesn't cower but is full of grace and life.

Putting others' interests ahead of our own starts by being alone in prayer. It is a supernatural mind-set and thus must be Holy Spirit powered. Opening to the Holy Spirit is the only way for us to receive a humility that puts others ahead of ourselves. Today bow your heart, and yield your thoughts to God. Ask Him to show you who to put ahead of yourself, and invite His Spirit to do a deep and abiding work in you to free you to love others today.

PRAYER

Father, Your ways are not my ways, and they sometimes feel out of reach to me. Show me today, Holy Spirit, how You can empower me to put others first in my journey. Amen.

Day 7

Serving Brings Blessing

Have this attitude in yourselves which was also in Christ Jesus, who, although He existed in the form of God, did not regard equality with God a thing to be grasped, but emptied Himself, taking the form of a bond-servant, and being made in the likeness of men. Being found in appearance as a man, He humbled Himself by becoming obedient to the point of death, even death on a cross.

PHILIPPIANS 2:5–8

Jesus towers over history and humanity. He is fully God and fully man. He is the Creator and sustainer of the earth, yet He took off His godhood and put on manhood. For what? For us! He wanted us to see Him not in His majesty but in His humility. He became a bond servant.

To a Greek person who lived in Philippi, the idea of being a bond servant was totally degrading. Greeks had a strong sense of freedom and the personal dignity that comes with freedom. These people had a violent hatred of bondage; they scorned and rejected slavery. Yet Paul chose this word "bond-servant," or *doulos*, to describe Jesus—a word on the surface that brought with it shame. Yet Paul described himself as the "bond-servant of Christ Jesus" in Romans 1:1. He obviously believed that complete and total surrender to his King was not only not shameful but also a huge blessing.

The thought of slavery is so distasteful that most of us could not imagine calling ourselves a slave of Christ's. But the Bible uses this imagery of slavery often, because it has been said that nearly one in every three people in the Roman Empire was a slave. When Jesus' disciples argued about who was the greatest, He told them, "It is not this way among you, but whoever wishes to become great among you shall be your servant, and whoever wishes to be first among you shall be your slave [*doulos*]" (Matt. 20:26–27). The Bible teaches that we are slaves to whatever we give ourselves over to. We once gave ourselves to wickedness and were enslaved by it. Now we are to give ourselves to Jesus, and we will live in holiness: "Just as you used to offer yourselves as slaves to impurity and to ever-increasing wickedness, so now offer yourselves as slaves to righteousness leading to holiness" (Rom. 6:19, NIV).

Jesus became a slave to free us from slavery! Then He asked us to give ourselves to Him and become servants, or slaves, to others—to give up our lives so we can get them back, to die to ourselves and live to Him, to find that serving Jesus and others is a blessing and the journey to real life.

PRAYER

Holy Spirit, change my thinking. I was taught that having others serve me meant that I was important, but You teach the opposite. You say that when I serve others and put them ahead of myself, then I am living and operating as You did, as a servant of all. Amen.

DAY 8

Worship and Service

Through Him then, let us continually offer up a sacrifice of praise to God, that is, the fruit of lips that give thanks to His name. And do not neglect doing good and sharing, for with such sacrifices God is pleased.

HEBREWS 13:15–16

Thankfulness can be hard to come by when life gets tough. It is easy for us to take our eyes off Jesus and put them on our circumstances. When we do that, thankfulness swiftly departs. But God wants us to offer up not just praise; He wants "a sacrifice of praise." A sacrifice of praise begins, as this verse says, as "the fruit of lips that give thanks to His name." Hearts that go deep with the Father must learn that thanksgiving is a key to worship and praise, to rising above our situations into His presence.

Worship always costs us something. Worship is about giving—expressing our hearts to God, giving ourselves to God, giving praise to God. Throughout the entire Bible it is clear that giving and worship go together. Everything about God has to do with giving, sharing, and helping, and He asks us to live this way too as an expression of worship.

Our culture, on the other hand, most often reflects an attitude of taking. Everything is about us, not others. Unfortunately, we have all been impacted by the attitude that to have is greater than to give. But Jesus said the opposite. He said, "It is more blessed to give than to receive" (Acts 20:35). Nehemiah understood this well. This is why he "sat down and wept" when he heard the report from Jerusalem: "Those who survived the exile and are back in the province are in great trouble and disgrace. The wall of Jerusalem is broken down, and its gates have been burned with fire" (Neh. 1:3–4, NIV). His heart was moved over the needs of others, and God used him powerfully to restore the people of Israel.

Greatness is found in blessing God and serving others, not in indulging ourselves. Today ask yourself if you are thankful to God in your circumstances. Are you offering Him a sacrifice of praise? Ask yourself if you hunger to serve others and put them ahead of you. Do you find ministering to others to be an exciting way to change lives? You should–God has blessed us to bless others. Humility will lead you to a worshipful heart and greatness for your King.

PRAYER

Father, teach me how vital worship is to my life in You. Teach me to take time to honor You and declare Your greatness. Help me realize that worship means giving of my time, talents, and resources to serve You and bless others. Holy Spirit, fill my heart with a spirit of generosity and praise. Thank You! Amen.

DAY 9

Honoring Those in Authority

David arose and cut off the edge of Saul's robe secretly. It came about afterward that David's conscience bothered him because he had cut off the edge of Saul's robe. So he said to his men, "Far be it from me because of the LORD that I should do this thing to my lord, the LORD's anointed, to stretch out my hand against him, since he is the LORD's anointed." David persuaded his men with these words and did not allow them to rise up against Saul. And Saul arose, left the cave, and went on his way.

1 SAMUEL 24:4–7

We all have people in our lives who are over us at some point or place, people whom God has allowed to be in positions of authority. Some of them are thoughtful and life giving, and some are not. Having a lousy boss or a teacher who is a dictator is no fun. Saul was just such an authority in David's life.

When Saul wandered into David's cave, David's men encouraged him to take Saul's life, but David wouldn't. What he did do, though, was cut off a piece of Saul's robe to make a point to Saul that he could have killed him. But later we are told that "David's conscience bothered him," and he realized that he had violated God—not Saul but God. David's words reveal his heart: "Far be it from me because of the LORD that I should do this thing to my lord, the LORD's anointed, to stretch out my hand against him, since he is the LORD's anointed."

When the apostle Paul was being questioned before the high court in Jerusalem and the high priest struck him in the face, Paul railed against the priest, and look at the outcome: "The bystanders said, 'Do you revile God's high priest?' And Paul said, 'I was not aware, brethren, that he was high priest; for it is written, "You shall not speak evil of a ruler of your people"'" (Acts 23:4–5). Paul, like David, knew that he had crossed a boundary with the Lord in speaking out against the high priest.

What do we do with leaders who dishonor us and make our lives miserable? We remember that kingdom values outweigh human values. When we honor even those who dishonor us, we position ourselves to be used by Jesus in a powerful way. This takes prayer and surrender to the Father's heart. It takes Holy Spirit–given love for those we don't even like. But this is our journey.

Today if you find yourself underneath a person you loathe, bow your heart, and pray for that person and yourself. Ask the Holy Spirit to make the most of the situation for His glory and your growth. He can turn a horrible and unhappy circumstance into a tool that you will be glad He used in your life.

PRAYER

Jesus, I don't like my situation or my leader. Please cause my heart to trust in You. Teach me patience and kindness in the midst of dishonor. Thank You, Lord, that You lived with unjust leaders and flourished among them. Remind me that in You I can do the same. Amen.

Day 10

Drawing a Line

Daniel made up his mind that he would not defile himself with the king's choice food or with the wine which he drank; so he sought permission from the commander of the officials that he might not defile himself.

DANIEL 1:8

Daniel made up his mind"—literally, he resolved or determined that he would not cross a line that others had. How many times have we crossed a line we knew we shouldn't but haven't said anything? What was it about Daniel, a teenager, that enabled him to stand up when so many times we don't? The Hebrew words say that Daniel set, or established, his inner self or heart—his inclination or loyalty—not to be polluted, desecrated, or stained. He literally guarded his heart. "Above all else, guard your heart, for everything you do flows from it" (Prov. 4:23, NIV).

When we don't guard our hearts, we compromise what we know is right and settle for far less than God wants. Then later we wonder, *What happened? Where did my passion go? My love for God and others is gone, but I have no idea why*. We didn't guard our hearts. We watched movies we never should have watched. We participated in conversations we knew weren't healthy. We crossed lines and quietly allowed things to stain our souls, spirits, and hearts.

How did Daniel succeed? He set a line ahead of time; he determined in advance what he would and wouldn't do. He surely knew that saying no could very well cost him his life. But to preserve his integrity and purity before God, he decided that he wouldn't cross that line. He feared God more than men.

When I fail similar tests, it is usually because I fear people more than God. That's not smart, but it's very human. This is why it is crucial for us to take time out every day to sit with Jesus and talk, read the Word of God, and allow convictions to build inside us. Jesus put it this way in Matthew 7:24: "Everyone who hears these words of Mine and acts on them, may be compared to a wise man who built his house on the rock." Our time alone with Jesus is a time to build our foundations—the convictions we will live out of each day. As we read His words, we need to pray over the things we read, being honest with Jesus about our fears, weaknesses, and failures. Then we need to invite the Holy Spirit to give us the grace to live out what we read and do what's right and not what's safe and comfortable.

This is what Daniel did. And he wasn't alone. His three friends held the same beliefs. People in our day hold these beliefs too. Don't believe the enemy when he calls you a fool and compares you to those who cross lines into wrong behavior. He hates the reality that you know what's godly and what's not.

PRAYER

Father, it is time for You to build deep convictions in me. Please convince me that Your words, not those of others, will bring me life. Teach me to build my house on You and Your Word. Amen.

Day 11

Guard Your Mind and Your Heart

Nabal answered David's servants, "Who is this David? Who is this son of Jesse? Many servants are breaking away from their masters these days. Why should I take my bread and water, and the meat I have slaughtered for my shearers, and give it to men coming from who knows where?" David's men turned around and went back. When they arrived, they reported every word. David said to his men, "Each of you strap on your sword!" So they did, and David strapped his on as well.

1 Samuel 25:10–13, NIV

Conflict is easy to find and hard to deal with. The crazy pace of our lives often sets us on a collision course with others who, like us, are far too busy to be thoughtful. The rush steals our margins and leaves us vulnerable to conflict. But Jesus encourages us over and over to be patient and kind with others, to love them even when they don't love us.

David's men had been thoughtful and life giving to Nabal's workers, but when David asked for Nabal's help in return, Nabal turned him away unjustly. And David was offended. When his men told him what Nabal had said, David said to them, "Each of you strap on your sword!" Far too often we are like David with Nabal.

Rather than bowing our hearts to Jesus and asking Him to mend us, we strike back at people who have wounded us.

The problem isn't that we get offended by others, because we all do. The problem is that we let the offense go deep within us so that we begin to lose our minds and hearts, and then we are in danger. So much pain could be avoided if we would just stop our emotions and reflect, pray, and wait. That doesn't release our tension or allow us retribution, but it does get us to a place where the Holy Spirit can work in us. When David became offended with Nabal, he lost one of his greatest strengths—self-control—and endangered his destiny.

A couple years ago I wrote a reactionary e-mail to a good friend of mine who had wounded me. I was just about ready to push the "send" button when I felt this little nudge from the Holy Spirit saying, "Ask Gale." *No way*, I thought. *I am totally justified in my feelings.* "Ask Gale . . . ask Gale . . . ask Gale." So I read the letter to my wife, Gale. She told me, "You don't want to send that letter. You love that guy, and you'll ruin your relationship with him forever if you send him that. Take the high road and call him. Go meet with him and hear his heart." Wow. I humbled myself and did what she suggested, and the relationship was saved, much to my great joy today.

Take time today to allow the Spirit of God into all your interactions with others. You will be glad you did.

PRAYER

Jesus, I surrender my heart to You today. I want Your way in all my interactions with others. Please remind me to slow down, not speed up, when I am offended. I hunger for You to direct me in a life-giving way today. Thank You, Lord! Amen.

Day 12

Breaking Pride with Kindness

Jesus . . . got up from the meal, took off his outer clothing, and wrapped a towel around his waist. After that, he poured water into a basin and began to wash his disciples' feet, drying them with the towel that was wrapped around him. . . . "Now that I, your Lord and Teacher, have washed your feet, you also should wash one another's feet. I have set you an example that you should do as I have done for you."

JOHN 13:3-15, NIV

Shortly before this stirring moment when Jesus washed His disciples' feet at what is known as the Last Supper, the disciples were arguing about which of them was the greatest—who would sit in the place of power when Jesus ruled as King. It is hard to imagine that this didn't feel like total failure to Jesus, who had spent the last three years teaching His closest followers about putting others ahead of themselves. He had done so many miracles and had cried and prayed over them, and they still failed miserably. Now, during His last night with them, rather than being angry at their short-sighted selfishness, Jesus operated in the opposite spirit of what they were doing. He did something so dramatic and tangible that it broke the spirit of selfishness that had His disciples in bondage.

Jesus didn't just tell the disciples to serve others; He demonstrated to them how to humble themselves to serve others: He washed their feet. There was no pretense, no show for dramatic effect—no need for that. Jesus, the King of the universe, stooped down and took a towel and washed away their sin and shame, their guilt and pride. All their imperfections were manifest in those dirty feet, all that would mar them and make them useless for the kingdom, the dirt of the world, the wrong thinking, the pride and arrogance of wanting to rule over others instead of serve them. Jesus took a towel and a basin and began to wash it all away.

He would soon go to the cross, and there He would not use a basin or a towel but rather His body and His blood to wash us clean. There He would break the bondage of our selfishness and set us free so that we could serve and love others as He intended us to from the beginning of time.

The lowly, loving spirit Jesus demonstrated that night is in desperately short supply today. That is why He told the disciples when He was finished, "Now that I, your Lord and Teacher, have washed your feet, you also should wash one another's feet. I have set you an example that you should do as I have done for you." This is my calling, and it is yours too if Jesus is your King. Serve Him by washing others' feet. Break the spirit of pride and selfishness with a spirit of humility and kindness. Don't allow others' thoughts and actions to dictate how you will love them. Love them as Jesus loved you when He washed you with His blood.

PRAYER

Jesus, how easy it is for me to forget what living with You is about. Serving You and others, worshiping You and loving people. Holy Spirit, fill me with a servant heart so that I too will wash others' feet. Amen.

Day 13

When We Don't Understand

Jesus replied, "You don't understand now what I am doing, but someday you will."

John 13:7, NLT

The occasion of this statement was the night before Jesus' crucifixion, at the Last Supper. Jesus had gotten up, put a towel around His waist, and headed straight for Peter to begin washing the disciples' feet. But why Peter first? Jesus' action was an expression of humility that would surely catch all the disciples by surprise, but none more than Peter. Jesus knew that Peter's pride and high self-reliance would struggle under His servant touch. And sure enough, Peter declared, "You shall never wash my feet" (John 13:8, NIV).

Peter's loud and boisterous response is easy for us to criticize, but the truth is, we all have moments like this with Jesus—times when we are sure that we know what God is up to and then find out that we are completely wrong, times when we mistake the heart and character of God for that of a man. But God tells us otherwise: "'My thoughts are not your thoughts, neither are your ways my ways,' declares the Lord. 'As the heavens are higher than the earth, so are my ways higher than your ways and my thoughts than your thoughts'" (Isa. 55:8–9, NIV).

All of us must admit at times that we have no idea what God is up to. Sometimes it seems that He intentionally loses in a situation that we thought He had to win. Sometimes it appears that He even works against Himself. It seems absurd, but it is totally God. He will allow us to end up in situations that are completely overwhelming, and then He will ask us to be still and quiet. He will pull the rug out from under us and remove all supports and then ask us to trust Him. These situations are so difficult that it is beyond our comprehension that God could be in them. But He is, and He is saying kindly to us, "You don't understand now what I am doing, but someday you will."

We must be careful to judge what we cannot understand, because God is often up to something far greater than we realize, and He needs our complete trust to accomplish it. That will require us to still our hearts and our thoughts. In these moments, allow God to show you what He has for you. Don't waste energy guessing or trying to figure Him out. Set your own wisdom aside, because what you see Him doing may contradict what you know He has promised you He would do. Be still and trust Him; listen to Him, and obey what His Spirit tells you to do. Do as Peter learned to do: "Cast all your anxiety on him because he cares for you" (1 Pet. 5:7, NIV).

You may not understand what God is doing now, but someday you will. Remember, He promised never to leave us or forsake us. Hang on to that, and watch for Him to surprise you with life as He did when He went to the grave and all appeared lost.

PRAYER

Jesus, I can't know what You are doing much of the time. Teach me to be still and trust You, no matter how dire my situation appears to me. Amen.

Day 14

God's Perspective

I came to Jerusalem and was there three days. And I arose in the night, I and a few men with me. . . . I did not tell anyone what my God was putting into my mind to do for Jerusalem and there was no animal with me except the animal on which I was riding. So I went out at night by the Valley Gate . . . inspecting the walls of Jerusalem which were broken down and its gates which were consumed by fire. . . . The officials did not know where I had gone or what I had done; nor had I as yet told the Jews, the priests, the nobles, the officials or the rest who did the work.

Nehemiah 2:11–16

Make no mistake, Nehemiah got his secret midnight strategy for examining Jerusalem's walls from God, for God also works alone and in secret. This seems foreign to most of us. Why not work in broad daylight? Why not engage others in the work? The walls of Jerusalem had been broken down for 141 years; people knew this rubble well. So why the stealth approach? Because anyone can look at broken-down walls or lives, but seeing what God sees is completely different.

The Holy Spirit moves in the people of God the way Nehemiah did in Jerusalem. He is quiet and often overlooked. He moves slowly through our journeys, touching our motives, revealing our hearts, exposing and assessing our debris. As with the walls in Jerusalem, many of us go on for years and years never really dealing with our broken-down situations. But then God moves through our wounded feelings and unforgiving hearts, looking to repair the damage. He comes like Nehemiah did, "inspecting." This word comes from an interesting Aramaic word, *sabar*, which means to "look to, i.e., have a confidence that a beneficial event will occur, implying dependent trust (even relationship) in the object of the hope."[1] God does exactly this in each of us. He searches us and sees the damage and destruction life has dealt us, and then, when we allow Him to, He confidently begins the deep work of repairing us.

Many of us miss out on this kind of supernatural movement of God because we are afraid to be real about our broken parts. When we've exposed our weaknesses to people in the past, we have experienced rejection, so we are certain that God will reject us too. But this word *sabar* expresses the heart of God, showing us that He has "a confidence that a beneficial event will occur." God believes that our rubble and pain can be turned to good, that it can actually be beneficial to us and those around us if we will allow Him to rebuild it.

Bow down, give in, and ask, like David did, for God to search you and know you today: "Search me, O God, and know my heart; try me and know my anxious thoughts; and see if there be any hurtful way in me, and lead me in the everlasting way" (Ps. 139:23–24).

PRAYER

Father, the thought of this secret work You do deep inside people often feels so threatening to me. Forgive me for not trusting that You are good and that You have only good in mind for me. Today please begin to rebuild the walls of my life, in the name of Jesus. Amen.

Day 15

Stop Sinning

King Nebuchadnezzar, please accept my advice. Stop sinning and do what is right. Break from your wicked past and be merciful to the poor. Perhaps then you will continue to prosper.

Daniel 4:27, NLT

There is a ton of wisdom in Daniel's advice to King Nebuchadnezzar: "Stop sinning and do what is right." Both the Old and New Testaments talk at length about repentance. John the Baptist spoke of it before Jesus arrived, and when Jesus taught, He spoke of it often. The disciples' main message in the book of Acts was "Repent and turn to the good news." The good news was Jesus, His healing life, and His restoring death and resurrection.

Today we rarely talk about repentance. The truth is, most of us are not even sure what it means. The word "repentance" comes from *metanoia*, two Greek words put together. *Meta* can mean "after," and *noia* comes from the root word *nous,* or "mind." Literally, this word originally meant "the mind afterward" or, as we say today, an afterthought. Repentance sure can quickly become an afterthought—something we really don't want to deal with. But God asks us to repent because He is trying to keep us from hurting ourselves or others around us. When repentance becomes an afterthought, we end up in danger.

Over time this word *metanoia,* like many words in our culture, changed meaning. It came to mean a significant changing of one's mind. Now that is something we can all use on a daily basis: a changing of our minds, a breaking of our old thinking, a fresh look at life and relationships. This is what the Holy Spirit does when we invite Him into our journeys and spend time with Him each day. Romans 12:2 speaks specifically about this when it says, "Be transformed by the renewing of your mind" (NIV). When we pray, read the Word, and worship God, the Holy Spirit will actually enter into our hearts and minds and encourage adjustments. He restores us and redirects us into life-giving purpose. He asks us to repent from things that kill us and moves us into His purpose for our journeys.

The latter part of Daniel 4:27 talks about what happens after we repent: "Break from your wicked past and be merciful to the poor." If we change our minds, we will also change our living. We will begin to care for others in ways we have never been inclined to before. Daniel's suggestion was way out of the king's thinking. The king was known for a lot of things, but caring for the poor was not among them—and that was exactly the point. Daniel knew that if the king opened to the heart of God, he would think and act differently.

Take time to allow the Holy Spirit to search you and show you where you need an adjustment in your thinking and living. Invite Him to show you how today can be new, fresh, and life giving.

PRAYER

Father, I am in serious need of some changing in my thinking. But honestly, I am not sure where that adjustment needs to take place. I only know that the way I live doesn't align with Your calling nearly as often as I wish it did. Touch me today. Renew my mind, and refresh my thinking and living. Amen.

Day 16

Defeating Pride

"King Nebuchadnezzar, please accept my advice. Stop sinning and do what is right." . . . Twelve months later [Nebuchadnezzar] was taking a walk on the flat roof of the royal palace in Babylon. As he looked out across the city, he said, "Look at this great city of Babylon! By my own mighty power, I have built this beautiful city as my royal residence to display my majestic splendor."

Daniel 4:27-30, NLT

We have a word at Water of Life for King Nebuchadnezzar's attitude in rejecting Daniel's advice: "stupid." Unfortunately, the king's kind of thinking is all too real for us. We know what is right, but we are often blinded by pride. Pride is so deeply fostered in our culture that it just feels normal, but pride kills. It destroys lives and destinies. In this case it cost the king his kingdom.

Jesus warned against pride over and over, encouraging us to see humility as a blessing that opens rivers of life rather than a curse that puts us at the bottom rung on the ladder of life: "Those who exalt themselves will be humbled, and those who humble themselves will be exalted" (Matt. 23:12, NIV). Unfortunately, no matter how much we work at being humble, it is a losing battle. Deep inside us is a well of pride just like the king's, and, try as we may, we cannot defeat that poison.

Only the Holy Spirit's graceful and powerful touch can win this battle. In Galatians 5:17 Paul explains this: "The sinful nature wants to do evil, which is just the opposite of what the Spirit wants. And the Spirit gives us desires that are the opposite of what the sinful nature desires. These two forces are constantly fighting each other, so you are not free to carry out your good intentions" (NLT). A battle is going on inside each of us between our flesh and God's Spirit, and Paul says that "these two forces are constantly fighting each other."

This is a frustrating war, but there is a way out. In Galatians 5:16 Paul tells us, "Walk by the Spirit, and you will not carry out the desire of the flesh." The Greek word for "walk," *peripateo*, is two words combined: *peri* and *patos*. *Peri* means "around," and *patos* means "to tread." Simply put, *peripateo* means to tread around. It has an old Hebrew meaning to it: to tread around in order to take possession of the land. It is what God told Israel to do in Joshua 1:3: "Wherever you set foot, you will be on land I have given you" (NLT).

To defeat pride and win the battle with our flesh, we must allow the Holy Spirit to have territory inside us—to "tread around" in us. We must invite the Spirit to freely search us and conquer our flesh so that we can live out of His power and not our own. Yielding to the Spirit and allowing Him to empower us is a daily journey. Let God walk around inside you. It will bring life and peace deep inside your spirit.

PRAYER

Holy Spirit, I need You to walk around inside me and conquer my pride and the desires of my flesh. Today I invite You to have Your way in me. Thank You for the peace and life You impart when I yield to You. Amen.

Day 17

The Key to Powerful Praying

Confess your sins to each other and pray for each other so that you may be healed. The earnest prayer of a righteous person has great power and produces wonderful results.

James 5:16, NLT

The earnest or effective prayer, literally the prayer that works, that comes from a person who is right with God, or more literally innocent, has great power. For many of us, that would seem to leave us out. We look at our lives, our thoughts, and some of our actions, and we immediately think, *My prayers most likely go nowhere.* In actuality this verse says that our prayers can be not only effective but also powerful, and they can produce "wonderful results." How?

The verse begins by saying, "Confess your sins to each other and pray for each other so that you may be healed." James is telling us to begin our prayers with confession, to God and others. If we hide our sin, our prayers lack power, because hell is watching all of us and always tempting us to stumble so that we cannot partner with God powerfully and effectively. If Satan can keep us hiding our sin in darkness, we will go through life powerless to make a difference. But if we decide to bring what is hidden into the light, God will take our failures and heal us. He uses what was meant for evil for His good.

Confession requires transparency and honesty with a person we trust, a person who loves God and wants God's best for us. When we confess our sin to our Father, we are forgiven, but when we bring our sin into the light by sharing it with another person, we get healed, restored, and redeemed anew. Once confession happens, the verse goes on to tell us to "pray for each other." Together we pray for the healing we need, and then we can intercede for others with powerful effectiveness.

It is no accident that these two concepts are so closely tied together in this one verse. We have to confess our sin in order to become righteous, or innocent. Our confession opens us up to the blood of Jesus washing us clean and making us, as Isaiah said, "white as snow" (Isa. 1:18), totally clean before God and empowered by the Holy Spirit to intercede with great power that produces wonderful results.

If your prayers seem weak and ineffective, ask the Holy Spirit for revelation. Ask Him to show you if there is hidden sin in your heart that needs cleansing before you can be effective in prayer. If He shows you clearly that you have an issue, find a brother or sister, a pastor or leader, and get it taken care of so the Holy Spirit can refresh and empower you as you pray.

PRAYER

Holy Spirit, search me, and know my heart. Please show me if there is anything in me that keeps my life from being all You desire it to be. If there is, please cleanse me and renew Your power in me. Amen.

Day 18

Willful and Weak

Why have you despised the word of the Lord *by doing evil in His sight? You have struck down Uriah the Hittite with the sword [and] have taken his wife to be your wife.*

2 Samuel 12:9

We humans are interesting, aren't we? We can be so bright and engaging, and just moments later we can be deceptive and dark. David was a brilliant man and an extremely gifted human being, but he was 100 percent human nonetheless. He had every fault that you and I have, and he handled some of them in a less than stellar fashion. Yet he loved God, and he was deeply loved by the Lord. This should give each of us something to think about. The fact that we are human and weak, sinful and stupid doesn't keep Jesus from loving us.

After David sinned with Bathsheba, he covered up his actions. But his cover-up was dark and deadly: he intentionally had Bathsheba's husband killed in a battle in order to protect himself. It is one thing to fall in our weakness, and it is yet another to cover it up willfully and intentionally. God treats these two sins differently. Weakness is just that—weak—but willfulness is turning our hearts against the Holy Spirit and *choosing* to run to darkness. Fear, insecurity, and pride drive us away from Jesus and into willful sin, just as they drove David. Because of his choices, David lost so much. He lost the child Bathsheba bore him, and later he lost two other sons. He also lost anointing and authority in the spiritual realm.

Lying and deceit can never heal what we have broken by our sin. Only the blood of Jesus can heal us. Hebrews 9:14 declares this: "How much more will the blood of Christ, who through the eternal Spirit offered Himself without blemish to God, cleanse your conscience from dead works to serve the living God?" We must figure this out if we are to live fully for Jesus. He died to heal us. He is extravagantly in love with us, and we would do well to run to Him when we fall and fail. No matter how bad our sin is, Jesus wants access to our mess. Hiding never brings life or healing. It only allows the enemy to continue to torment us.

James 5:16 tells us how to get the healing we need: "Confess your sins to one another, and pray for one another so that you may be healed." When we confess our sins to our Father, we receive forgiveness; but it is when we confess our sins to our brother or sister that we receive healing from the bondage of shame. So if you find yourself trapped, find a friend or pastor you can trust, and tell him or her the truth. It will free you and heal you and restore your heart.

PRAYER

Jesus, thank You that You died so I could live. I hunger to live in freedom, not bondage. Please teach me to come to You and not hide when I have fallen. Forgive me for my weakness and willfulness. They both draw me away from You. Amen.

Day 19

Sin's Consequences

When a man came near . . . , he would put out his hand and take hold of him and kiss him. In this manner Absalom dealt with all Israel who came to the king for judgment; so Absalom stole away the hearts of the men of Israel.

2 Samuel 15:5–6

David had dreams. Many of them, like ours, were for his children. But what do we do when our dreams die—when the things we longed to see take place either in our own lives or the lives of our children don't happen? Or when those we love turn on us? This has probably happened to all of us at some point in our lives.

David's sin with Bathsheba opened his family to vast amounts of pain. His failures with women in general were his downfall, and his lust was passed on to his sons, who lusted for women and power. When David realized what he had perpetrated on his children, he was devastated. But in those moments when he was sinning, he didn't think about the cost to others, only the hunger of his flesh for himself.

David had dreamed of his son Absalom becoming king one day. But when his firstborn son, Amnon, raped his half-sister, Tamar, Absalom murdered Amnon. But even after this revenge killing, David still wanted Absalom to become king, because the young man had much of David's heart and leadership ability. Unfortunately, Absalom also had his father's lack of self-control at times, so waiting to become king was not something he really wanted to do. He took matters into his own hands and undermined his father, the king, in order to secure the throne. This led to a massive coup attempt, which forced David and those loyal to him to flee Jerusalem.

Heartbroken, David made his way out of the city, as 2 Samuel 15:30 describes: "David went up the ascent of the Mount of Olives, and wept as he went, and his head was covered and he walked barefoot." This is such a sad commentary on a great man. But it is our story too. When we make decisions in our flesh, the impact is far greater than most of us realize. We wound those we love and destroy our destiny for a moment of pleasure or power.

Stop and bow your heart. Remind yourself that your time alone each day with the Lord is your safeguard against poor choices. Ask Him to guard both your heart and your mind in Christ.

PRAYER

Father, today put Your hedge around my heart. Guard me from foolish ambition and wrong, hurtful choices. Thank You that Your plans for me are for life, not death—plans for a future and a renewed hope. Amen.

Day 20

Confession Brings Light

"O Lord our God, you brought lasting honor to your name by rescuing your people from Egypt in a great display of power. But we have sinned and are full of wickedness. . . . O my God, lean down and listen to me. Open your eyes and see our despair. . . . We make this plea, not because we deserve help, but because of your mercy. O Lord, hear. O Lord, forgive." . . . I went on praying and confessing my sin and the sin of my people.

DANIEL 9:15–20, NLT

Confession changes everything. It rights wrongs and makes straight our crooked living. It opens the doors for God's kingdom to come and His will to be done. Confession allows God to correct and renew us and build a strong foundation under our shifting lives. As Daniel said, "We have sinned." He was speaking of the Jews in Jerusalem, but it's true for all of us. The sooner we get comfortable with confession, the happier we will be, because confession admits the truth, and that aligns us with Jesus, who is the truth. It positions us to receive new life, eternal life.

Without confession we withdraw into our reality: sin. We grow proud and self-willed. Our hearts grow hard, and our lives dry up. We buy the lie, the mirage, that life is better on our own terms than on Jesus' terms.

The Bible is pretty clear about how God sees sin and people. Romans 3:10–23 says,

> "No one is righteous—not even one. No one is truly wise; no one is seeking God. All have turned away; all have become useless. No one does good, not a single one." "Their talk is foul, like the stench from an open grave. Their tongues are filled with lies." "Snake venom drips from their lips." "Their mouths are full of cursing and bitterness." "They rush to commit murder. Destruction and misery always follow them. They don't know where to find peace." "They have no fear of God at all." . . . For everyone has sinned; we all fall short of God's glorious standard. (NLT)

Most of us would prefer to skip these verses when we read our Bibles, but they are vitally important to our well-being in Jesus. They are like a measuring tape. We may say, "Well, I don't commit murder; I really don't see myself as that bad," but these verses describe the human condition over time and history: we are violent, broken, and in need of a Savior. They set a framework for why we need Jesus' blood—why we need confession, repentance, and humility.

Confession teaches us that God is amazing and kind, forgiving and all-knowing when it comes to our shortcomings but also that He never moves away from us. Yes, the verses are dark, but they help us see how much light Jesus actually brings to people who confess their shortcomings and agree with Him.

PRAYER

Jesus, You are amazing! You know how wicked I can be, and yet You are never ashamed of me or my weaknesses. Thank You, Lord, for the light You shine every day into my darkness. Teach me to enjoy confession, because it opens the door to forgiveness. Amen.

DAY 21

Jesus Prays for Us

I have prayed for you, that your faith may not fail.

LUKE 22:32

Jesus prays for us! For some of us that is truly difficult to imagine. He stands with us when we cannot stand. Often when things are going well, we stand on our own power, thinking, *I've got this*, and without realizing it we leave God out of the equation. But when we cannot stand, most of us run to Him. Even when we run to Him out of weakness and fear, He never turns us away. He stands with us even when we cannot stand—even when we fall.

When Jesus told His disciples that He prayed for them, He understood more than they did that they were human and prone to fail. So He prayed that in the fire their faith would hold fast. This prayer was specifically targeted toward Peter, and many of us know that Peter had issues. He was hardheaded and sometimes overconfident, not in God, but in Peter. Then he would fail, and Jesus was always there to pick him up. This is what makes Jesus so amazing. He knows more about our weaknesses than we do, and they don't put Him off. More than that, Jesus prays for us just as He prayed for His disciples: "Who is to condemn? Christ Jesus is the one who died—more than that, who was raised—who is at the right hand of God, who indeed is interceding for us" (Rom. 8:34, ESV).

One of our greatest struggles is to overcome shame and the deep sense of failure when we fall. Peter was just like us, and Jesus was crazy about old Pete. He prayed for Peter, and He prays for us.

He loved Peter with all his faults, and He loves us in the same way. Jesus prays for us today, interceding for us, believing for us, just as He did for Peter.

Hebrews 7:25 tells us, "He is able also to save forever those who draw near to God through Him, since He always lives to make intercession for them." He lives to pray for us! He is indeed a strong tower, a refuge to run to when we are hurting or have fallen.

When we have friends who really get our journeys, friends who will stand with us, it makes all the difference in the world. Jesus is more than a friend—He is God! Don't run away. Run to Him, the One who lives to pray for you!

PRAYER

Jesus, You are beyond amazing. Your love for me is still as hot and on fire as it was for Peter. Remind me never to run from You but always to run to You. I hunger to get this, God. I want to know that You have me covered every day in prayer. Please, Holy Spirit, reveal to me today the Father's deep love for me. Teach me to pray for others, Jesus, like You pray for me. Amen.

Day 22

Remember What God Has Done

I said to them, "You see the bad situation we are in, that Jerusalem is desolate and its gates burned by fire. Come, let us rebuild the wall of Jerusalem so that we will no longer be a reproach." I told them how the hand of my God had been favorable to me and also about the king's words which he had spoken to me. Then they said, "Let us arise and build." So they put their hands to the good work.

Nehemiah 2:17–18

After all the years that the walls of Jerusalem had lain in rubble, how was it that Nehemiah could move the people to rebuild the walls? Surely and most obviously, the hand of God was on him. But to stop there would miss how strategic of a leader this man was. Nehemiah understood people, and he understood how to lead people. It was no small thing he did when he went in secret around the city assessing the situation and then consulting with God in prayer. But in addition to depending on the Spirit to guide him as a leader, Nehemiah also knew that what God had done for him in the past was a precursor for what He was going to do in the future. He knew that the favor God had given him with King Artaxerxes to get him back to Jerusalem was a supernatural story that would give hope to the people in the land who were hopeless.

Do you believe that God has worked and is working in your life not just for you but for others? Do you remember the great works that the Holy Spirit has done in you? Have you written them down in a journal so you won't forget the details? Journaling is a tremendous way to build faith. It allows us to look back and remember the details about how God has worked in our lives. Then we can share them with others who are stuck and in need of hope, just as Nehemiah did with the Jews of Jerusalem. People throughout time and history have loved stories, and if you know God, He has given you a story. Your story may seem mundane to you, but that is likely because you have failed to put the details on paper and forgotten how big God's hand was in the moments of your life.

Stop and take the time to journal your story, not just for yourself but for others. When you are down, open your journal, and read your writing. I have been doing this for thirty years, and my stories have changed my life. And if you attend Water of Life, my stories have likely also changed your life—not because they are my stories but because this is the way of God. Nehemiah's journey opened the door for his people's faith to grow, and your journey can do the same.

PRAYER

Jesus, You do incredible things in people who trust You. Please use my life and my story for Your glory! Thank You for all You have done in me. Remind me never to take my story for granted but to record it for others. Amen.

DAY 23

Change Your Mind

Offer your bodies as a living sacrifice, holy and pleasing to God. . . . Do not conform to the pattern of this world, but be transformed by the renewing of your mind. Then you will be able to test and approve what God's will is.

ROMANS 12:1-2, NIV

What motto or whose picture is on your T-shirt? What values do you conform to? In what ways do you reshape yourself in order to fit in with the people around you? What do you give yourself to as a kind of living sacrifice? Anything that claims that it can make us the greatest, most successful, or most famous can capture us and conform us to its own set of values.

A magazine ran a series of articles asking people, "How has your mind changed?" Some answered by telling how a relationship changed their racial prejudices or how some tragedy or suffering made them more aware of and compassionate toward others. What can change our minds? That is an interesting question. Changing people's minds is a difficult and rare thing, especially if the transformation means changing their directions, opinions, goals, and plans.

Yet such change is exactly what Paul calls every Christian to. He calls us to be completely transformed by the renewing of our minds. He calls us to give ourselves as living and holy sacrifices. Surrender is worship, and from surrender comes transformation.

Can anyone notice that your life is molded by the mind of Christ? Can anyone see your transformation? The changes in us should be noticeable to others. That was certainly the case for Daniel and his three friends in Babylon. They had devoted their hearts to the Lord in their youth, and the changes God had worked in their hearts before they were sold into slavery were decidedly visible as they underwent various tests in the service of foreign kings. How has your life of faith changed your mind? How have your priorities changed? Are you still conformed to this world, or is your mind being transformed? Can anyone notice the difference in you as you offer yourself more fully to God?

Think back to your mind-set before giving your life to Christ. What had you predetermined? What were you stubborn about? Be honest here, then listen, look back, reflect, and see what you have learned over the past weeks, months, or years since you began walking with Jesus. You may be surprised to find that you are being transformed as you journey into the Father's heart.

PRAYER

Holy Spirit, lead me to see differently, think differently, live differently from how I did before knowing You. I need transformation, and You are the transformer. Reset my priorities. Transform my mind—and my life! Amen.

DAY 24

Being Perfected

Let patience have its perfect work, that you may be perfect and complete, lacking nothing.

JAMES 1:4, NKJV

If there is anything I like to pray less for, it is patience. I know that when I pray for patience, I will get an opportunity to exercise my prayer quickly. Having said that, I do pray for patience sometimes, because patience isn't a virtue I possess a whole lot of. Patience is necessary, particularly if you live in a crowded setting such as Southern California, like I do. The freeways will teach you patience, the store lines will teach you patience, and the doctor's office will certainly teach you patience. Or will they?

Each of has a choice to make daily: will we learn and grow, or will we just growl our way through each day?

James tells us to let patience have her perfect work. What does that mean? The word "perfect" is *teleios*, a Greek word that comes from *telos*, meaning "end." *Teleios* has to do with finishing things, maturing things, completing things. It has to do with God completing His work in us—bringing us to perfection, making us whole and complete as He intended us to be when He created us. The opportunity to practice patience is one of the tools He uses each day to mature us. That is tough today when we all spend far too much time hurrying from one appointment or event to the next.

The Greek word for "patience" is often translated "endurance," or "patient enduring," as well as "perseverance." It means staying in and not giving up, not allowing our flesh to take over our days when we are crowded and rushed. Circumstances will strain us nearly every day, but the Holy Spirit can empower us to put others first and do it joyfully. It is when the Spirit takes over our feelings and empowers us that patience begins to complete its work in us—the work that Jesus began on the cross.

Over and over the Bible tells us to be patient and allow the Spirit to work. When we are not patient, we do not grow in Him:

> Live a life worthy of the Lord and please him in every way: bearing fruit in every good work, growing in the knowledge of God, being strengthened with all power according to his glorious might so that you may have great endurance and patience. (Col. 1:10–11, NIV)

Once we are yielded to God and begin to allow His Spirit to work deeply in our lives, our growth will take time. We will need to be still and wait. Waiting is a key to growing with Jesus, and yes, it takes patience. In our hurried and hectic world, being still seems to have no value. Waiting can feel like wasting time, but waiting is really the key to letting patience have her perfect work in us.

PRAYER

Jesus, I am so impatient, and I see that my impatience cuts off Your Spirit's work in me. Forgive me. Holy Spirit, teach me to wait and, while I am waiting, to remember that I am not wasting time but investing in eternity. Amen.

Day 25

Rich Toward God

About this time some of the men and their wives raised a cry of protest against their fellow Jews. They were saying, "We have such large families. We need more food to survive." Others said, "We have mortgaged our fields, vineyards, and homes to get food during the famine. . . . We must sell our children into slavery just to get enough money to live. We have already sold some of our daughters, and we are helpless to do anything about it, for our fields and vineyards are already mortgaged to others." When I heard their complaints, I was very angry.

NEHEMIAH 5:1–6, NLT

Money exposes both selfishness and generosity. It is able to clarify motives and completely destroy convictions. It can bring life, and it can bring death. It is all about perspective: is the money yours or His? The Jews in Jerusalem were living in a time of famine, and the financial pressure they were under uncovered the motives of many of them. Their neighbors had taken advantage of them in a time of need, even to the point of buying their children for slaves, because their families were starving. Desperate times can tell us a ton about ourselves.

Jesus knew what greed can do to people. That is why He warned us in Luke 12:15, "Beware, and be on your guard against every form of greed; for not even when one has an abundance does his life consist of his possessions." This is an astounding statement if we step back and assess it: Jesus, the Son of God, the King of kings, tells us to beware and be on our guard. Now if I told you to beware, you might perk up for a few minutes and listen, but if Jesus tells us to beware and be on our guard, we'd better listen, because He never makes a statement like that unless He's onto something big.

And He *is* onto something big here: selfishness. If we are human, we have it. We all have it. We are about ourselves. We were born about ourselves, and many of us go through life about ourselves, never considering others' needs around us. But Jesus said, "Not even when one has an abundance does his life consist of his possessions." He then went on to tell a story of a man who had a huge farm and built bigger barns to keep his stuff—he was selfish. Then this man died, and all his stuff was gone. Then Jesus said, "So is the man who stores up treasure for himself, and is not rich toward God" (Luke 12:21).

"Rich toward God"—what a thought. No matter how much money we have or don't have, we can all be rich toward God if we will put Him first in our hearts. He will then teach us generosity and about living for others, not just ourselves. Make being rich toward God a priority in your daily living, and you will end up wealthy in His kingdom.

PRAYER

Father, I am selfish. Forgive me. I am often all about myself, but I don't want to live that way. Holy Spirit, You can heal me, so today I invite You to give me a hunger to be rich toward God. I want to overcome selfishness and bless others. Empower me to live that life. Amen.

Day 26

It All Belongs to Him

The earth is the LORD*'s, and all it contains, the world, and those who dwell in it.*

Psalm 24:1

When we come right down to partnership with God, it is important to understand what our role actually is. You and I are stewards. What is a steward? A caretaker. David, as leader over God's people, understood this. Despite the weaknesses and failings he exhibited at times, he knew that he had been called by God to care for His people and that he was responsible before the Lord for their care and well-being.

Jesus spoke about stewards in Luke 12:42–44:

> Who then is the faithful and sensible steward, whom his master will put in charge of his servants, to give them their rations at the proper time? Blessed is that slave whom his master finds so doing when he comes. Truly I say to you that he will put him in charge of all his possessions.

A steward then is a servant who oversees his or her master's stuff. Genesis 1:1 tells us that "God created the heavens and the earth," and that makes *all* the stuff His!

Stewardship started at creation. It is based on the concept that everything we have is God's, not ours. Our possessions have been given to us by God because ultimately everything was made by Him and belongs to Him, no exceptions. He created the carbon that was compressed into precious diamonds. He made the land we buy and sell. All our possessions, whether jewelry, gold, coins, land, cars, or buildings, came from His creative hand: "The earth is the LORD's, and all it contains, the world, and those who dwell in it." "All things come from You" (1 Chron. 29:14). When we see things in this light, it is the first step toward seeing stewardship the way God intended us to see it.

So if everything is God's, how do we wind up with what we have? As we have seen, James 1:17 answers that question: "Every good thing given and every perfect gift is from above, coming down from the Father of lights." Everything we have was given to us by our Father, who willingly and gladly gives to those who love Him. It is His nature to give. He doesn't hoard, and He isn't selfish or stingy. He is kind and generous, and He delights in blessing His kids.

If we get this, we will have a good perspective regarding our possessions. If, on the other hand, we don't see that God gives graciously to us, we will completely miss the concept of stewardship.

PRAYER

Father, You are generous and gracious. Teach me Your ways. I am prone to be selfish and a taker. Holy Spirit, give me a spirit of generosity with all I have. Thank You for desiring to build me into Your image. Amen.

DAY 27

Integrity

For the entire twelve years that I was governor of Judah . . . neither I nor my officials drew on our official food allowance. The former governors, in contrast, had laid heavy burdens on the people, demanding a daily ration of food and wine, besides forty pieces of silver. Even their assistants took advantage of the people. But because I feared God, I did not act that way.

NEHEMIAH 5:14-19, NLT

Living with integrity is not an easy thing to do in our day and age, when people scoff at morals and deride any approach that seems less than cutting edge. Integrity is considered old school. But for those who follow Jesus, integrity is the foundation God builds in us—the soil that brings forth life and destiny.

Unfortunately, many who declare that they love God don't live honest lives, thinking that somehow they will be covered by God's forgiveness and grace. God certainly does forgive us when we humbly turn to Him and own our lack of integrity, but we should always remember that 2 Chronicles 16:9 tells us, "The eyes of the LORD search the whole earth in order to strengthen those whose hearts are fully committed to him" (NLT). Being fully committed to God doesn't mean being perfect, but it does mean that we fear Him, not people, and this fear causes us to live with honesty deep inside. Nehemiah made this clear: "Because I feared God, I did not act that way."

When we fail to fear God first, our lack of integrity can disqualify us for an assignment that the Holy Spirit has for us. That surely would have been the case for Nehemiah if he had taken advantage of the vulnerability of the Jews in Jerusalem. Instead he rose above the accepted behavior and positioned himself to break the selfishness that was destroying the people.

For twelve years Nehemiah made it a point never to take the governor's food allowance, even though it was designated for him and his leaders. He had seen the Jews taken advantage of, and he wisely chose to live far from that kind of behavior. He paid for his food out of his own pocket because he saw that the people were already carrying a huge load, and his calling was to lighten their load, not add to it.

This kind of thinking that put God and others ahead of himself was what made Nehemiah a great leader. His love and concern for the welfare of others, his humility to serve alongside them, and his deep love for God all positioned him as a person who could be trusted by God and called on for a massive undertaking such as the one God had sent him to.

Real ministry, Holy Spirit–led ministry, hangs on the thin thread called integrity. Nehemiah understood this, and because of his integrity, he fulfilled his destiny. Living with integrity is difficult today, but it was difficult in Nehemiah's day as well. Decide now to live in the fear of the Lord and walk daily with integrity.

PRAYER

Father, please convict me when I compromise. I know I fear people over You sometimes, and I also know that it isn't life giving for me or those around me. Teach me to love You deeply and live daily with integrity. Amen.

Day 28

Pride Comes Before a Fall

Take a census of all the tribes of Israel—from Dan in the north to Beersheba in the south—so I may know how many people there are.

2 Samuel 24:2, NLT

Why do we humans hunger for power? Something in us drives our flesh to be better or stronger or more beautiful than others. What is that? It corrupts the Spirit of God in us. It derails our destinies and sets us up for painful failure, as it did with David. It is called pride. The Hebrew word for "pride" in the Old Testament has to do with lifting oneself up. That is what David did when he took a census of the tribes of Israel, and it is what we all do when we become prideful.

"Count the people" for David meant "How strong are my armies?" It was all about power and control. But Jesus is never about power and control. He is always about life and encouragement, hope and healing, defeating darkness and delivering others. He is all about humility. He was never ashamed to be humble. He found humility to contain great strength. Pride, on the other hand, drives us to seek others' approval and puts us in vulnerable places with others.

The book of Proverbs has much to say about pride and power corrupting our lives: "When pride comes, then comes dishonor, but with the humble is wisdom" (Prov. 11:2), and, "Pride goes before destruction, and a haughty spirit before stumbling" (Prov. 16:18). When pride grips us, dishonor is around the corner, and destruction is on the way. We stumble badly, as David did in ordering a census. Humility, on the other hand, is the way of Jesus. Everything about Jesus was humble, from His birthplace in a barn to His parents' low economic means, which prevented them from even being able to sacrifice a lamb in the temple commemorating their thanksgiving for Jesus' birth.

Jesus was the picture of humility, always deferring to His Father's will and desire, often doing this openly in order to teach us how to live. As Andrew Murray says in his book on humility, "Jesus was nothing so His Father could be everything."[2]

Today if you are embarrassed to consider yourself humble or live a humble lifestyle or engage in a spirit of humility each day, ask the Holy Spirit to change your thinking. We can never take on the likeness of Jesus unless we do as Peter tells us in 1 Peter 5:5: "All of you, clothe yourselves with humility toward one another, because, 'God opposes the proud but shows favor to the humble'" (NIV).

PRAYER

Holy Spirit, today I ask You to clothe me in humility. Teach me that humility isn't a thing to fear but in fact positions me for greatness in the Father's kingdom. I bow down to You today, Lord Jesus, and ask for Your heart of humility to be born deeper and deeper in me. Thank You, Lord, for doing Your work in me. Amen.

Day 29

God's Word—Our GPS

All the people assembled . . . just inside the Water Gate.
They asked Ezra the scribe to bring out the Book of the Law of
Moses. . . . Ezra the priest brought the Book of the Law before the
assembly. . . . He faced the square just inside the Water Gate from
early morning until noon and read aloud to everyone who could un-
derstand. . . . Then they bowed down and worshiped the LORD *with*
their faces to the ground. . . . They read from the Book of the Law of
God and clearly explained the meaning of what was
being read, helping the people understand each passage.

NEHEMIAH 8:1-8, NLT

The promises, purposes, and person of God are found only in the Word of God. So is the plan we need for living in the heart of God. We cannot grow in the Lord without the Bible.

Nehemiah hungered for his people to be made whole again, for their lives, like yours and mine, to reflect the hope that God imparts to those who know Him. Nehemiah knew it was impossible to know God well without knowing His Word, so he asked Ezra the priest to read the Word over the people and explain it to them. When they heard the Word, they worshiped God, and they grew. This is God's plan for us—to hear the Word, respond to it, and grow: "As newborn babes, desire the pure milk of the Word, that you may grow thereby" (1 Pet. 2:2, NKJV).

The Bible was written over approximately fifteen hundred years by more than forty different authors from kings to peasants, shepherds to tentmakers. Yet all these authors, who were on three different continents, wrote with agreement on what are some of the most controversial subjects in our world today.

Over and over the Word of God expresses God's love for us and how He wants to call us to Himself. It is our GPS for life—our road map to help us find our way in this journey:

> The whole Bible was given to us by inspiration from God and is useful to teach us what is true and to make us realize what is wrong in our lives; it straightens us out and helps us do what is right. It is God's way of making us well prepared at every point, fully equipped to do good to everyone. (2 Tim. 3:16–17, TLB)

The Bible was written by the Holy Spirit, and it is the Holy Spirit who teaches us from it as we sit in His presence and read it. John 14:26 tells us, "The Helper, the Holy Spirit, whom the Father will send in My name, He will teach you all things, and bring to your remembrance all that I said to you." Each time you open your Bible, invite God's presence into your time with Him, and He will instruct you, heal you, correct you, and equip you with all you need for the day.

PRAYER

Holy Spirit, give me a hunger for Your presence and Your Word. Teach me Your heart as I set myself before You today and read Your Word. Correct my wrong thinking, and feed me with the Father's heart today. Amen.

Day 30

The Joy of the Lord

Nehemiah the governor [and] Ezra the priest . . . said to them, "Don't mourn or weep on such a day as this! For today is a sacred day before the LORD your God." For the people had all been weeping as they listened to the words of the Law. And Nehemiah continued . . . "Don't be dejected and sad, for the joy of the LORD is your strength!"

NEHEMIAH 8:9–10, NLT

The Bible has an amazing ability to reflect our hearts to us and give us a glimpse of what God sees inside us. Usually that view is not as pretty as most of us have imagined in our mind's eyes. We may see a reflection of selfishness, greed, and ambition. Sometimes we see anger and unforgiveness. At other times we recognize unbelief and how far we have moved from our Father's heart. Each of these scenarios has one thing in common: the deep sadness that can overwhelm us when we come to grips with the truth about ourselves.

But this sadness can become a road back to life in Jesus if we choose to walk it with Him. Paul explains:

> The kind of sorrow God wants us to experience leads us away from sin and results in salvation. There's no regret for that kind of sorrow. But worldly sorrow, which lacks repentance, results in spiritual death. Just see what this godly sorrow produced in you! Such earnestness, such

> concern to clear yourselves, such indignation, such alarm, such longing to see me, such zeal, and such a readiness to punish wrong. (2 Cor. 7:10–11, NLT)

Sorrow is not something many of us hope to experience, but godly sorrow has an incredible ability to lead us away from sin. Sin causes a different kind of sorrow—a worldly sorrow that kills us. But the sorrow that comes from God brings forth life and hope and healing deep within us. When this sorrow touches us, God intends us to bow low and invite His Spirit's healing touch. This repentance reconnects our hearts to our Father's heart. The grace of the cross then comes to us, and God's presence is restored in us.

But we need not stay in a place of sorrow, beating ourselves up. As Nehemiah and Ezra told the people of Jerusalem, we should not "mourn or weep on such a day as this." We should let the Spirit of God do the work of sorrow in us and then move on in the grace and hope of Jesus. No need to dwell in sorrow; once we have allowed its work of grace to touch us and bring us back to our Father's heart, we can move on. It is not our feelings of sorrow that heal us but the work of Jesus on the cross. His healing and hope are free gifts for us to embrace and celebrate.

Let the words of Nehemiah fill your heart today: "Don't be dejected and sad, for the joy of the LORD is your strength!"

PRAYER

Father, as much as I dislike the sorrow I feel when Your Word reveals my heart, I pray that I would embrace it. Use this sorrow to correct me and heal me, and then release a new and deep joy within me today. Amen.

Days 31–60

Passing God's Test So He Can Use You

God's goal with us in tests is often not the test itself
or helping us get through it
but seeing how we handle the journey.
God will test us—
the question is, will we pass?

Day 31

God's Tests

Daniel spoke with the attendant who had been appointed by the chief of staff to look after Daniel, Hananiah, Mishael, and Azariah. "Please test us for ten days on a diet of vegetables and water," Daniel said. "At the end of the ten days, see how we look compared to the other young men who are eating the king's food. Then make your decision in light of what you see."

Daniel 1:11–14, NLT

Tests are never fun. God tests us, Satan tempts us, and the world tries us. But while Satan and the world care nothing about us, God is crazy about us. We might ask, "Why would He test us then?" The tests God puts before us are tools that cause us to grow into greater usefulness. Daniel faced as many tests as anyone we see in the Bible, and through them his life deeply impacted the culture in which he lived. That culture was so demonic and dark, so wicked and hurtful, that it seemed impossible that it could be moved. Yet Daniel moved kings and culture, because he passed his tests.

Notice that Daniel asked for ten days of testing. That is important. The number ten in the Bible represents faithfulness. We see this in the Ten Commandments (see Exod. 20), in giving 10 percent of our money (see Mal. 3:10; "tithe" means a tenth), in the disciples praying for ten days in the Upper Room waiting for Jesus to move (see Acts 1:13–14),[1] and in believers enduring ten days of persecution (see Rev. 2:10). Testing and faithfulness go hand and hand. God will test us—the question is, will we pass?

Daniel was tested by the Babylonian culture, which was dark and demonic. We are tested by our culture, which is growing darker by the day! Paul wrote about this in 1 Thessalonians 2:18: "We wanted to come to you—certainly I, Paul, did, again and again—but Satan blocked our way" (NIV). Satan loves to impede us, but God uses obstacles to grow us.

> So [the attendant] listened to them in this matter and tested them for ten days. At the end of ten days their appearance seemed better and they were fatter than all the youths who had been eating the king's choice food. So the overseer continued to withhold their choice food and the wine they were to drink, and kept giving them vegetables.
>
> As for these four youths, God gave them knowledge and intelligence in every branch of literature and wisdom; Daniel even understood all kinds of visions and dreams. (Dan. 1:14–17)

Notice that after Daniel passed the test, God opened new doors for him. God does this for us. It is easy for us to kick and scream and flail when we are being tested. Instead, stop and ask God to pour out His grace to help you pass the test. He will do it. He is crazy about you, and He wants to use your life to impact our culture for His glory. Be still and yield, and God will move you through.

PRAYER

Father, Your tests are sometimes hard to see, and I miss the test and flunk. Please teach me, Holy Spirit, to be still and listen when life gets hard. Teach me to yield to You, Father, so I can pass the test. Amen.

Day 32

A Bad Report

In late autumn . . . in the twentieth year of King Artaxerxes' reign, I was at the fortress of Susa. Hanani, one of my brothers, came to visit me with some other men who had just arrived from Judah. I asked them about the Jews who had returned there from captivity and about how things were going in Jerusalem. They said to me, "Things are not going well for those who returned to the province of Judah. They are in great trouble and disgrace. The wall of Jerusalem has been torn down, and the gates have been destroyed by fire."

NEHEMIAH 1:1–3, NLT

The bad news he received from Jerusalem sent a shock wave through Nehemiah. We have all experienced something like this, haven't we? Life is rolling along, and suddenly we get a bad report of news we never wanted to hear: a loved one is lost, a friend is sick, an accident has happened. Life is full of bad reports. None of us likes them, but all of us have to endure them.

What do you do when you receive word of something that sends shock waves through your heart and life? Do you anxiously look about you for a friend to support you? Do you grow angry and feel that life is unfair? Is bitterness just around the corner from you, one bad report away?

Isaiah 41:10 is a verse we can all embrace in a time of need: "Do not fear, for I am with you; do not anxiously look about you, for I am your God. I will strengthen you, surely I will help you, surely I will uphold you with My righteous right hand." For most of us, our first response to a bad report is fear. But fear is not the answer to a bad report; faith is. News that shocks our spirit is like a barometer; it gives us a reading on what we really believe and who we trust. But we should think of it as a test, because it often is. When you hear bad news, do you run to God or others? Does bad news cause you to pull away from your Father's heart, or does it drive you into His presence?

When your spirit is shocked and you are struggling, stop and ask the Holy Spirit to search you and reveal your hidden thoughts and fears so you can bring them to your Father. Don't run from Him in a time of need; run to Him. He is your answer, a strong tower and a safe refuge in the time of need. News that blows us up never shakes Him. He is a rock, a fortress, and He is never surprised or shaken. He knows that no matter how painful and life changing the news is to us, He can take what is painful and crushing and somehow, some way, use it for our good and others' growth.

PRAYER

Father, when I get news that shakes my world, I want my first response to be "Help me, Father." I pray that You will teach me to lean on You in times of plenty and in times that are lean, when the news is good and when it is bad. I want my life to reflect a deep trust in You. Holy Spirit, please build in me a deep trust in You. Amen.

Day 33

Will You Keep God First?

It came about in the month Nisan, in the twentieth year of King Artaxerxes, that wine was before him, and I took up the wine and gave it to the king. Now I had not been sad in his presence. So the king said to me, "Why is your face sad though you are not sick? This is nothing but sadness of heart." Then I was very much afraid. I said to the king, "Let the king live forever. Why should my face not be sad when the city, the place of my fathers' tombs, lies desolate and its gates have been consumed by fire?" Then the king said to me, "What would you request?" So I prayed to the God of heaven.

Nehemiah 2:1–4

Nehemiah had been elevated to one of the highest positions in the land—cupbearer to the king. As a captive slave, this was likely far beyond what he could ever have imagined. This was no accident; it was his destiny. Yet in this position of prominence, Nehemiah was tested by God.

Nehemiah could never have risen to the position of cupbearer without being highly trusted. It was his job to protect the king from being poisoned by others. The person in this position had to be handsome, cultured, knowledgeable in court procedures, and able to converse with the king and advise him if asked. The cupbearer was a man of great influence, which he could use for good or evil.

The king Nehemiah served was the most powerful man on Earth during his reign. King Artaxerxes was no mythological character; he ruled over a kingdom that spread from the border of China to the Mediterranean Sea. Yet Nehemiah never lost his perspective. He knew that his place in life had been ordered by his God, not his king. This kept him from giving way to fear when the king noticed his sad face and heavy heart—something he had never allowed the king to see before. Nehemiah looked to God in his moment of truth, and his faithfulness allowed him to be used by God to rescue the Jews.

Do you find yourself in a place that is part of your destiny? You may feel stuck, marginalized, and discounted, or you may be elevated to a high place, leading many people. It really doesn't matter, as long as it is where Jesus wants you. This is where you will learn the lessons of life that can only be taught by the Holy Spirit. This is where God will test you and see if He can trust you to keep Him first before He uses you for all He destined you for.

Our positions may not appear powerful to others, but all that matters is that we have said yes to God and that He is guiding our lives each day, moment by moment. Today ask God to get you where He wants you to be and to use you for His glory beyond your wildest dreams.

PRAYER

Father, I hunger for more of You. I want to be where You want me to be, doing what You created me to do. Teach me patience to wait as You build me. Teach me to trust as You meet with me. Fill my life with Your presence and Your glory today. Amen.

DAY 34

Defeating Your Giants

David said, "The LORD who delivered me from the paw of the lion and from the paw of the bear, He will deliver me from the hand of this Philistine." And Saul said to David, "Go, and may the LORD be with you."

1 SAMUEL 17:37

During his years as a shepherd boy, David learned to sit alone with the Lord and worship. It was in these years that he began to write his first songs, or psalms, to the Lord, and it was in these years that he began to build faith—a faith that would be tested not only by lions and bears but also by the giants God would allow in his life.

David was confronted with various giants in his life, but early on he learned not to panic when he faced them. Goliath epitomized the subsequent line of "lions and tigers and bears" that would challenge David's life. Amazingly, each time David was confronted by an enemy, he did not allow fear to overwhelm him. He had faith in the Lord—a faith that is possible for each of us who is willing, like David, to sit at our Father's feet and allow His Spirit to teach us His ways. David's giant-slaying faith was built alone in worship with his Father in heaven.

The British preacher Martyn Lloyd-Jones wrote, "Faith is a refusal to panic."[2] David's faith was surely tested when he faced a lion for the first time, and I am certain that when he came face to face with a bear, his heart began to beat out of his chest. Yet in these two victories and his many victories to come, he chose to believe that the defeat of his enemies was God's deliverance manifested in his life. No panic. No matter how great the challenges, David trusted God.

It seems impossible to believe that you and I could also face the giants in our lives and not panic. But remember, David didn't start with Goliath. He began with the subtle, small challenges of life, just as we do. Then, as he passed each test, his faith grew, and so did the peace of God over his life. None of us just arrives at a place where we are eager to take on a Goliath in our lives. No, we are tested and retested. We must first conquer the daily circumstances that trip us up and the relationships that pester us. Then, when we pass the test, our faith will grow. When we don't give way to panic but instead invest in lots of prayer, suddenly, one day when God unleashes a Goliath on us, we will be not only ready but also eager.

The next time you are confronted with lions and tigers and bears, remember David. He did not panic but trusted in the Lord, and his faith grew. David had tremendous trust in the Lord; he knew that God would deliver him. You have the same God David did. Trust Him, and His deliverance will manifest in your difficulty and deliver you from the hand of any giant that comes along your path.

PRAYER

Lord, make me a person who will choose You in stressful situations. Keep me from panic, and help me to trust in You. Help me to remember David when I am confronted with the challenges in my life. Amen.

Day 35

Kindness Under Fire

Daniel spoke with the attendant who had been appointed by the chief of staff to look after Daniel, Hananiah, Mishael, and Azariah. "Please test us for ten days on a diet of vegetables and water," Daniel said.

DANIEL 1:11–12, NLT

One of the things that made Daniel an amazing man and leader was his disposition—his kindness under fire. Even when he was being tested, he was nice! I am not usually nice when I am being tested; how about you? It is easy to get grumpy and grouchy, sore and mean when we are walking through tough situations. Tests can try our patience.

Proverbs 17:3 says, "The refining pot is for silver and the furnace for gold, *but the LORD tests hearts.*" When we are being tested, it is always easiest to focus on getting *through* the struggle and just getting it over with, but Daniel made the journey count. Even in the fire he was nice. God's goal with us in tests is often not the test itself or helping us get through it but seeing how we handle the journey. Do we grow angry and sore? Do we get impatient and edgy? Or do we settle into the hand of God and rest in the test? Daniel trusted that God's best was there for the taking if he would just journey with Him.

Romans 5:3–4 says, "We also glory in our sufferings, because we know that suffering produces perseverance; perseverance, character; and character, hope" (NIV). That is what God is after in our tests—character that grows in the midst of suffering, which gives birth to perseverance, which brings forth hope. Hope is what it takes to live, and Daniel could easily have had none in his circumstances. He was a slave in a dark, dark place, but he thrived in that place with the hope he gleaned from the tests he passed. He kept his thoughtfulness intact by not reacting to the test but by responding to the Spirit.

When we are tested, we can quickly feel fear, confusion, and frustration if we don't stop and pray. If we are not still and don't take the time to quiet our hearts, we can develop negative attitudes. Daniel kept still. He spoke thoughtfully, even asking his overseer, "Please test us." The "please" word is revealing of Daniel's heart. We see this attitude over and over in Daniel, a kindness that contradicted his circumstances. Such an attitude is built into a heart that has surrendered to Jesus by the power of His Spirit brooding over us and softening us in our tests.

At times staying kind in a trial seems impossible, but nothing is impossible with God! We are all going to be tested. The test itself is not what counts but rather how we respond in the test.

PRAYER

Father, teach me to yield to You in the test. I need to constantly be reminded that You are for me and that You love me even in the test. I pray for Your Word and Your Spirit to speak deeply to me in the tests I face today. Amen.

Day 36

God's Sovereignty

The king became indignant and very furious and gave orders to destroy all the wise men of Babylon. So the decree went forth that the wise men should be slain; and they looked for Daniel and his friends to kill them.

Daniel 2:12–13

There are times in all our lives when other people's decisions impact us—decisions we don't agree with and wish had never been made. But they impact us whether we like it or not, whether we deserve it or not, and whether we are prepared for the repercussions or not. Whether it is a parent, a boss, or a politician who decrees that his or her latest rule or law is really for our benefit, when others make bad decisions for us, we can quickly and easily lose sight of the overarching hand of our heavenly Father. Is God really good? Is He in control? At times like these we can doubt it. We wonder how a good God could let someone who doesn't know us impact us in a negative way. Why isn't He guarding and protecting us?

The sovereignty of God is an immense and daunting concept for some of us to consider. How could God be in charge of every situation going on throughout the earth at the same time? How could He actually personally care for individuals who are impacted and blown up by the decisions of others?

Make no mistake, the Bible is clear about the fact that God rules over His kingdom. In Matthew 6:10 Jesus told us to pray for

His kingdom to come and His will to be done "on earth as it is in heaven," but we often don't feel His will being done when others' decisions impact our journeys. Sometimes we lose sight of what God is doing in our circumstances, particularly when things impact us in negative ways. Rather than believing the best, believing beyond ourselves, we give in to despair and lose faith, but the Bible teaches us that God uses everything for good when we trust Him: "We know that in all things God works for the good of those who love him, who have been called according to his purpose" (Rom. 8:28, NIV).

God being sovereign doesn't mean that life won't be tough. It doesn't mean that others won't make decisions that impact our lives in negative ways. "The dictionary defines 'sovereign' as '1. Paramount; supreme. 2. Having supreme rank or power. 3. Independent: a sovereign state. 4. Excellent.' None of these definitions mean that God controls everything."[3] In other words, God doesn't force people to make good decisions. Clearly He gives us a choice to participate in the work of His kingdom or not. That is why Jesus told us to pray for His kingdom to come (see Matt. 6:10).

That is exactly what Daniel and his friends did. Rather than despair and fall into depression and surrender to the king's decree, they prayed for God to move in the decree, in the negative decision impacting them—and He did. He will do the same for you today if you will run to Him when life gets hard.

PRAYER

Father, when others negatively impact me, remind me not to give in to their decisions but rather to pray, to believe that You can work in me and my destiny in spite of their actions. Amen.

Day 37

God Reigns over People

Then Daniel went to his house and informed his friends, Hananiah, Mishael and Azariah, about the matter, so that they might request compassion from the God of heaven concerning this mystery, so that Daniel and his friends would not be destroyed with the rest of the wise men of Babylon.

Daniel 2:17–18

We often think that since God is supreme, nothing can happen without His approval. That isn't what the Bible teaches. In 2 Peter 3:9 Peter wrote, "The Lord is . . . not wishing for any to perish but for all to come to repentance." God doesn't want people to perish, but they do. Clearly people have a choice in destiny and eternity.

While people have the freedom to act against God's will, we also have the freedom to choose our responses when others make decisions that impact us negatively. Daniel could have surrendered his heart and faith when the king gave orders for all the wise men, including Daniel and his friends, to be killed. He had done nothing wrong, yet this all-powerful king who'd had a disturbing dream (see Dan. 2:1) on a whim had decreed that all the wise men, or counselors, should be killed.

Instead of panicking or expecting the worst, which I am pretty sure most of us would have done, Daniel went to his house, got his friends, and prayed. Daniel and his friends turned to God when the king's decree impacted them wrongly. By doing this they created the possibility for God to rule and reign over their situation, to move personally and intimately with them. They found God's plans for them to be as Jeremiah had written: "'I know the plans I have for you,' declares the LORD, 'plans to prosper you and not to harm you, plans to give you hope and a future'" (Jer. 29:11, NIV). Their faith unlocked the door for this wicked king to see the sovereign hand of God in his own circumstances, and that opened the door for God to move Daniel and his friends into places of influence and power in order to bring life and hope to perishing people.

What if they hadn't prayed? What if they hadn't believed that God was good and moving with power in their circumstances and instead focused on how they were being impacted in such a negative way? We will never know, but I am certain of this: you and I are feeling the pressure of others' decisions today, and what we do with that pressure will determine how much Jesus can move in our situations with power.

Stop and pray. Believe. Don't give up or give in to despair because of decisions that others around you are making. Remember, God doesn't control every decision people make, but God is still in control. "Whatever the LORD pleases, He does, in heaven and on earth, in the seas and in all deeps" (Ps. 135:6).

PRAYER

Father, today others will impact me, and I will also have opportunities to impact others. I pray, Holy Spirit, that You will empower me and remind me not to give in to unbelief and discouragement but to pray and press through to see You move with power. Amen.

Day 38

Mocking Voices

When Sanballat heard that we were rebuilding the wall, he became furious and very angry and mocked the Jews. . . . "Can they revive the stones from the dusty rubble even the burned ones?"

NEHEMIAH 4:1–2

Sanballat was just one man. He had likely been the governor over Jerusalem before Nehemiah showed up, so he was a powerful man, but he was just one man. Unfortunately, one person is often all it takes to sidetrack us from a joyful walk with the Lord—just one man or woman who stands against us, who dislikes us, who may, like Sanballat, be furious or angry with us. Such a person can wreck our journeys and dash our hope.

Faith can be a fragile thing. When it is a seedling, it can be quickly swept away in its tender early years. Hell knows this and makes sure that our faith is tried. Remember when Jesus spoke to Peter about Satan wanting to sift him? "Simon, Simon, behold, Satan has demanded permission to sift you like wheat; but I have prayed for you, that your faith may not fail" (Luke 22:31–32). The one thing Jesus said that He prayed for was Peter's faith—because it was still so fragile. But as faith takes root and matures, it can become a giant that towers over obstacles and angry people.

If we lose our faith, we lose everything. We lose our desire to pray, our hope, our vision, and Satan knows this well. That is why we will all come up against angry people who mock us and look on us with scorn. Just when we are hopeful that God could actually make something out of our rubble, the enemy tries our faith and discourages us from believing that God can do His great healing work in us.

Don't surrender to the voices of others, no matter how powerful or angry they may be. God has spoken His promise over you and your life. He will take those old dry and dead bones and put life back in them. He will revive you and restore you, just as He restored the walls of Jerusalem.

> The LORD . . . set me down in the middle of the valley; and it was full of bones. . . .
>
> He said to me, "Son of man, can these bones live?" And I answered, "O Lord GOD, You know." . . . Thus says the Lord GOD to these bones, 'Behold, I will cause breath to enter you that you may come to life . . . and you will know that I am the LORD.'" . . . So I prophesied as He commanded me, and the breath came into them, and they came to life and stood on their feet, an exceedingly great army. (Ezek. 37:1–10)

Satan's greatest fear is that God's people will resist him and that God will then revive them into a great army that will build His kingdom and destroy the work of the enemy. This is what God is working in us today. Joyfully yield to Him, and watch your faith grow.

PRAYER

Father, can You really take all the mess in my life and revive it? It seems impossible to me, because I know how faithless I can be. But today, Holy Spirit, I invite You to grow my faith so that it will withstand all the enemy brings against me. Amen.

DAY 39

Don't Take It Personally

We built the wall and the whole wall was joined together to half its height, for the people had a mind to work. Now when Sanballat, Tobiah, the Arabs . . . heard that the repair of the walls of Jerusalem went on, and that the breaches began to be closed, they were very angry. All of them conspired together to come and fight against Jerusalem and to cause a disturbance in it. But we prayed to our God, and because of them we set up a guard against them day and night.

NEHEMIAH 4:6–9

It is easy to focus on people when they attack us, and why not? Their words and actions wound us. Their attitudes impact us. It is personal, and it is about us! Yes, it is personal, and it is about us, but not on the terms we often embrace. The book of Nehemiah is about people like you and me who struggled to get through each day until a spiritual man came into the picture and challenged them to live for something bigger than themselves. Nehemiah asked them to believe that their God could do a great work in them. But to do this, they had to forget about themselves and the personal attacks against them.

When we embrace the heart of the Father, we have to lose ourselves. Hell will attack us, and the enemy will use people like

Sanballat and Tobiah to wear us down and discourage us. This has been going on for hundreds of years, and the only people who rise above it are those who decide that the battle isn't about them. It is about Jesus, their Savior and their King. It is about Him and all He desires to do to touch this world and the people around us.

Hell attacks us personally because the devil knows that doing so is the easiest and quickest way to get us to take our eyes off the goal. That is why what we are going through always seems bigger than what other people are dealing with—our boss is the worst, our children are the most difficult, our spouse works the longest hours. Our problems make us lose perspective! But our problems are not our problem; what we *do* with our problems is our problem!

Nehemiah 4:9 tells us that Nehemiah prayed; it was his habit to go to God in prayer when things were tough. It needs to be our habit to go to God. He is so amazing at helping us regain the perspective we've lost. His Spirit restores balance in our lives. It is His job to fight our battles, not yours or mine. When the enemy comes and makes it personal, it is an attack, not an accident; it is meant to cause you to lose perspective. But don't. Instead, stop and pray. Don't wait. Don't run to your friends. Go to your Father, and ask Him to restore to you His perspective in your journey.

PRAYER

Jesus, remind me today and every day that this is Your battle, not mine. My part is to run to You and allow You to cover me and battle for me. Remind me that the struggle is about You way more than it is about me. Amen.

DAY 40

Never Trapped

Give me relief from my distress; have mercy on me and hear my prayer.

PSALM 4:1, NIV

As a pastor, I have often spent time with families who were experiencing huge crises. Whether it was parents losing a child in a car accident, someone finding out that a loved one has a brain tumor, or a wife discovering that her husband has three completely blocked arteries in his heart and must have open heart surgery immediately, these situations have been desperate for relief. The stress has been so high and the pain and uncertainty so deep that all these people could do was cry out for relief. Most of us have been here before, and if we haven't, we will be one day.

Life is full of crisis, and crisis can drive us into our Father's heart or out of His presence. How we react to crisis will be determined not by our circumstances and how dire they are but rather by how much we have previously decided to lean into God in good times and in bad times. If we see each minor crisis during our days as an opportunity to yield to God and trust Him, we will put roots down deep into His heart—roots that will hold fast in a later crisis:

> Blessed are those who trust in the LORD and have made the LORD their hope and confidence. They are like trees planted along a riverbank, with roots that reach deep into the water. Such trees are not bothered by the heat or worried by

> long months of drought. Their leaves stay green, and they never stop producing fruit. (Jer. 17:7-8, NLT)

Hearts with roots that grow deep are hearts that seek after the Lord every day. They make it their life's aim to please Him and live in Him, to yield to Him in the big things and the small things of life. But too many of us turn to our loving Father's heart only when we are out of control and cannot alter our situations.

David had been in many circumstances that had squeezed him and threatened to choke off his life. When he cried for relief in Psalm 4:1, he was actually asking God to enlarge the space in his life. When crisis closes in, it can quickly corner us and crush our spirits. It can trap us and remove any and all choices we thought we had. This declaration, or cry, from David literally says, "In crisis you made space for me," or, as the King James Version reads, "Thou hast enlarged me when I was in distress."

When crisis closes in on you and you feel trapped and hopeless, bow your heart and quiet yourself. Anxiety and fear will not help you; stillness in the storm will. Turn to God, and cry out for Him to enlarge your space. Don't surrender to the feeling of being trapped. In God you are never without hope. He has the space you need to survive and succeed in every situation and circumstance.

PRAYER

Father, teach me to run to You with every situation, big and small. I want to learn to put my roots down deep so that when tough times come, I will not only survive them but, like David, I will learn to grow through them. Amen.

Day 41

Even If He Doesn't

Nebuchadnezzar said to them, "Is it true, Shadrach, Meshach, and Abednego, that you refuse to serve my gods or to worship the gold statue I have set up? I will give you one more chance to bow down and worship the statue I have made. . . . If you refuse, you will be thrown immediately into the blazing furnace. And then what god will be able to rescue you from my power?" Shadrach, Meshach, and Abednego replied, "O Nebuchadnezzar, we do not need to defend ourselves before you. If we are thrown into the blazing furnace, the God whom we serve is able to save us. He will rescue us from your power, Your Majesty. But even if he doesn't, we want to make it clear to you, Your Majesty, that we will never serve your gods or worship the gold statue you have set up."

DANIEL 3:14–18, NLT

"The God whom we serve is able to save us." This small statement reveals a vast treasure of life and faith. Daniel's three friends knew their God and His possibility to move with power to rescue them. They knew His deep love for them and His ability to do the miraculous, because He was the God they served, loved, and honored.

When we walk with Jesus, we build up a huge reserve of faith and trust, often without knowing it. This reserve comes from loving Him daily and allowing Him to love us. When we spend time in His Word, setting our hearts on His promises and building our houses on His life and not our own, we are transformed. Time with the Lord stabilizes us, brings His peace to bear on our situations, and enthrones Him over all our daily needs and cares. Then when the crisis comes, and it will, we will live out of His possibility, not our own. That is what happened with Shadrach, Meshach, and Abednego, Daniel's three friends. They didn't start living for God the day the king threw them into the fire. They had begun that journey years before, and when they were tested, they knew whom they believed.

Their second statement is even more telling: "But even if He doesn't, we want to make it clear to you, Your Majesty, that we will never serve your gods." "Even if." These men didn't have a shallow faith that said, "If God doesn't do what we think He should, we're out." No, they had a deep, intimate, and supernaturally imparted faith that enabled them to believe beyond their circumstances.

This is the faith we are all after—the faith that says, "My God is able. But 'even if' things don't turn out to my liking, I'm still all in. There is nowhere else to go but to Jesus." Nearly every day is a test—certainly a test smaller than a fiery furnace but a test nonetheless that will need a faith that says "even if." Open deeply and intimately to Jesus today, and He will establish His life in yours so that you can pass the test.

PRAYER

Father, I want a faith that says "even if," I will still follow You: even if I don't get my way, I'm in; even if things are hard, I'm in. Holy Spirit, impart Your heart to me; build in me a deep and life-changing faith today. Amen.

Day 42

When the Heat Rises

"We will never serve your gods or worship the gold statue you have set up." . . . So they tied them up and threw them into the furnace. . . . Shadrach, Meshach, and Abednego, securely tied, fell into the roaring flames. But suddenly, Nebuchadnezzar jumped up in amazement and exclaimed to his advisers, "Didn't we tie up three men and throw them into the furnace?" "Yes, Your Majesty, we certainly did," they replied. "Look!" Nebuchadnezzar shouted. "I see four men, unbound, walking around in the fire unharmed! And the fourth looks like a god!"

Daniel 3:18–25, NLT

The pressure put on Daniel's three friends to worship idols paints a stark picture of both my journey and yours. The world pressures us each day to bow down to it, conform to it, and live the way it lives. When we don't, we feel the heat—not a fiery furnace but the heat from others who dislike our unwillingness to bow down to the things they believe make the world turn.

The Bible has made it clear that Satan wants our worship, and he will continually pressure us to relent and bow down to him. We should never be surprised when we feel the pressure to conform and bow to the enemy. It's been this way since Satan himself fell, and he hungers for us to bow to anyone or anything but Jesus. He hungers for us to worship him.

> The devil took [Jesus] to a very high mountain and showed him all the kingdoms of the world and their splendor. "All this I will give you," he said, "if you will bow down and worship me." Jesus said to him, "Away from me, Satan! For it is written: 'Worship the Lord your God, and serve him only.'" (Matt. 4:8–10, NIV)

It takes courage to stand for our convictions and live out of our core values and to remain kind and love others well while doing it. We can do this, but not on our own. When God's Spirit is working in us and we are surrendering to Him, then kindness and strength merge together, and we find the grace to love well and still say no. In these times it is no longer us standing alone, hoping for a lifeline to save us from the pressure to conform to the world; no, it is Jesus. It is His strength and grace that move in us and through us.

"I see four men, . . . and the fourth looks like a god!" Well, that's because the fourth man was God! He was Jesus our King, and He always shows up at the right time, even though we often doubt that He hears us. Jesus showed up in the fiery furnace, and He will show up when the heat is on us! He will never leave us or forsake us. Live today with confidence that when the pressure builds, you don't need to panic; just pray and press into Jesus. He will show up, and, as He has always done, He will provide all you need.

PRAYER

Father, today when I feel the pressure to conform to the world, remind me never to bow down to other gods but to keep my heart and faith set on You and to know that You will rescue me. Amen.

Day 43

Brokenness Is a Tool for Building

David was playing the harp with his hand, as usual; and a spear was in Saul's hand. Saul hurled the spear for he thought, "I will pin David to the wall." But David escaped from his presence twice. Now Saul was afraid of David, for the LORD was with him but had departed from Saul. Therefore Saul removed him from his presence.

1 Samuel 18:10–13

Life often takes twists and turns that none of us sees coming. Certainly that was the case with David. He was doing what he had done for some time, playing the harp in the presence of the king, minding his own business, living as innocently as possible. Then out of nowhere Saul hurled his spear at David—not once but twice—and removed David from his presence. He fired him! Saul marginalized David, undermined him before others, and made his life miserable.

Have you ever been minding your own business when out of nowhere someone took issue with you? Attacked your person even though you had never provoked that person? Unjustly accused you? This situation with Saul caused a great deal of brokenness for David. He fled for his life, lost his friendship with Jonathan, and ultimately lost his wife. But it was all part of God testing and shaping him for something far greater than David could have imagined.

God uses brokenness to build us. I don't like it, and I'm guessing you don't either, but brokenness is often God's tool of choice to get deep into our business. Once He has our attention and our hearts are broken and humble, He does a deep work in us, an unseen work, something we would never have been open to otherwise but that is vital for our destinies.

I have met the Lord most deeply in times of brokenness. This is Jesus' way. The Lord lived a life of sorrow and dealt with much human brokenness: "He was despised and forsaken of men, a man of sorrows and acquainted with grief; and like one from whom men hide their face He was despised, and we did not esteem Him. Surely our griefs He Himself bore, and our sorrows He carried" (Isa. 53:3–4). God is compassionate, but He is wise not to heal us until all His work in us is complete.

Don't doubt His love for you when you are in deep brokenness. Run to God, and allow Him to comfort you. You can ask God for an explanation, for clarity as to the whys and wherefores, but He may be silent. He may not reveal what He is doing until some time later, after you have passed through the fire with Him. But when He is finished, rest assured that you will be grateful for His loving and wise guidance in your circumstances.

PRAYER

Father, in the midst of the fire, I cannot see my way out. I find myself at a loss as to how or what to pray. Please meet me here, Jesus. Thank You that You fully understand my pain, my loss, and my brokenness. There is no God like You, Lord. I am open to You. Please move according to Your will in my life. Thank You. Amen.

Day 44

Do Not Be Afraid

When I saw their fear, I rose and spoke to the nobles,
the officials and the rest of the people: "Do not be afraid of them;
remember the Lord who is great and awesome. . . .
Our God will fight for us."

Nehemiah 4:14–20

When life gets hard, we all need a man like Nehemiah who will remind us of what we know is true: "Do not be afraid. Our God will fight for us." That's so simple but so important. When we are attacked, how do we react? Do we take it personally? When we take it personally and get offended, we are of no use to the kingdom of God, because we are living for ourselves. It is only when we lose our lives that they can be multiplied back to us. It is only when we refuse to be offended that we can be effective for the King and the kingdom. This is why the book of Proverbs warns us not to be easily offended: "Good sense makes one slow to anger, and it is his glory to overlook an offense" (Prov. 19:11, ESV).

This is all about perspective. Nehemiah's words were simple but important because they brought perspective. When life gets hard, do we lose perspective quickly? Do we react with an attitude of abundance or one of poverty? How we react determines how we grow. An attitude of poverty is easy to recognize: "Poor me! Why me? Why not someone else?" An attitude of poverty kills God's promises and possibilities in us. It paralyzes us spiritually. It feeds fear and kills faith.

An attitude of poverty is what kept Israel out of the Promised Land for forty years:

> "We went in to the land where you sent us; and it certainly does flow with milk and honey, and this is its fruit. Nevertheless, the people who live in the land are strong, and the cities are fortified and very large. . . ."
>
> Then Caleb quieted the people before Moses and said, "We should by all means go up and take possession of it, for we will surely overcome it." But the men who had gone up with him said, "We are not able to go up against the people, for they are too strong for us." So they gave out to the sons of Israel a bad report of the land which they had spied out, saying, "The land through which we have gone, in spying it out, is a land that devours its inhabitants; and all the people whom we saw in it are men of great size. . . . We became like grasshoppers in our own sight, and so we were in their sight." (Num. 13:27–33)

This is a story we should all know well, a story of two mentalities: one of abundance that gave life and overcame giants and one that bred death and surrendered to poverty. When giants appear in your life, don't give into a poverty mentality. Stand strong, and be reminded, as Nehemiah reminded his people, that "our God will fight for us."

PRAYER

Father, I want to live in a mentality of abundance, not poverty. Teach me to trust You to fight my battles, and remind me that You are always victorious! Amen.

Day 45

Steady Under Pressure

When Daniel learned that the law had been signed, he went home and knelt down as usual in his upstairs room, with its windows open toward Jerusalem. He prayed three times a day, just as he had always done, giving thanks to his God.

Daniel 6:10, NLT

Daniel had an uncanny inner strength that allowed him, in one crisis after another, not to get blown up by the pressures surrounding his life. Most of us would have been so shaken and filled with drama upon hearing of a new law that anyone who prayed to God would be condemned to death that we would have lost our way. But rather than reacting to this law meant to wound and trap him, Daniel simply went home and did what was his habit to do: pray. He prayed, and he kept himself positioned, time after time, for God to move with authority in his circumstances.

Prayer can seem like an artificial crutch, something to run to when we are weak and overwhelmed, but that is foolish thinking. Prayer builds a foundation of faith in us that can overcome circumstances beyond our control. It enables us to yield our hearts and fears, along with our strong reactions, to God. Prayer positioned Daniel above his emotions in the middle of the battle. What made Daniel the amazing man he was wasn't something huge that none of us could ever achieve. It was simply his willingness not to react first but to pray first. He didn't argue about how unjust the decree was or force a confrontation to justify his prayers to God. He prayed and worshiped, believing that God could do the defending far better than he could.

Unfortunately, it takes a crisis to get many of us to pray. We tend to run on our own power until our worlds blow up, and then we run to God. Honestly, this is the way some of us learn how important prayer is, by running to God in a crisis. If it takes a crisis to get us on our knees, then let the crisis come. But once we have experienced God rescuing us, there is a better, deeper, and more mature way to live in Jesus: make praying and surrendering a daily habit. The reason Daniel prayed during his crisis is clear: "He went home and knelt down *as usual.*" In other words, prayer was his habit.

We don't need to pray at our windows three times a day as Daniel did, but turning to God throughout the day sure is a good habit. Stop at work, at school, during your day, and pause to reconnect with God, to give thanks for a conversation or a person you interacted with. Praise Jesus for leading and guiding you during the day. Remind Him how grateful you are for a living God like Him to care for you! Grow deeper in your prayer life, and watch your life grow wider and better each day.

PRAYER

Jesus, thank You for being there for me in the crisis and in the day-to-day stuff. Thank You for reminding me that You can make my day-to-day journey full of life and divine appointments if I will stay connected to You. Amen.

Day 46

Alone with God

After He had sent the crowds away, He went up on the mountain by Himself to pray; and when it was evening, He was there alone.

Matthew 14:23

Jesus, more than any of us, knew the value of being alone and praying—taking the time to find quiet and connect with God. Jesus was always with people, and He knew that in order to be effective in His Father's work, He needed to be alone.

Solitude is crucial for all of us, no matter what our occupation is. Time alone with God is an investment in eternity. It is never wasted time. It takes time to connect with God. It takes times of quiet to hear His voice and be able to deal with the deep issues we all face. It takes time to get refreshed by His Spirit. We should see this time as a privilege, not as a labor of love. When I take time away to be alone with God, a crazy and amazing thing happens: I find myself with thoughts like, *Nothing in the world matters except God. Nothing counts like being with Him and having Him be with me.*

Jesus said in Matthew 6:6, "Go into your room, close the door and pray" (NIV). When we get alone, deep life flows between our hearts and the heart of God. It is in quiet places where He explains life to us. It is in these places where He corrects and resets us. In Mark 4:34 we are told, "When he was alone with his disciples, he explained everything to them" (NLT). In the same way, when we are alone, Jesus explains things to us that we cannot learn anywhere else. When we are alone, He heals and restores us.

We need to practice being alone! We need to take time out of our busy schedules and sit with God. If we will stop and sit with Him, we will receive more than we could ever ask or think. It is when we do this that real devotion is grown—devotion to the things of God, devotion that comes from deep inside. This is not a surface thing but a deep life connection with God. This only comes when we take time alone with Him.

Prayer and devotion always go together. The Bible tells us in the book of Acts about a guy named Cornelius: "He was a devout, God-fearing man, as was everyone in his household. He gave generously to the poor and prayed regularly to God" (Acts 10:2, NLT). It is no accident that Cornelius was both generous and prayerful. I am fairly certain that Cornelius's prayer life and his devotion to God allowed the Lord to form a generous heart in him. I am also pretty certain that when you and I go alone with God and devote ourselves to Him, He will do the same thing in us. He will remove jealousy, envy, and greed and replace them with forgiveness, love, and generosity.

PRAYER

Holy Spirit, please call me to Yourself, and teach me to take time away from others to be alone with You. I want to grow in You, Father, and I understand that it takes time alone, away from the crowd. Please move in me to chase after You in my time alone with You. Amen.

Day 47

Don't Lose Your Mind

David arose and fled that day from Saul, and went to Achish king of Gath. But the servants of Achish said to him, "Is this not David the king of the land? Did they not sing of this one as they danced, saying, 'Saul has slain his thousands, and David his ten thousands'?" David took these words to heart and greatly feared Achish king of Gath. So he disguised his sanity before them, and acted insanely in their hands, and scribbled on the doors of the gate, and let his saliva run down into his beard.

1 Samuel 21:10–13

David was in a painful place, maybe similar to one you find yourself in today. Things just never seem to go your way. Life is hard and not getting easier. It's important to remember that sometimes this is from God. He allows painful situations in our lives at times to change our direction. Have you gone to Him with an open and honest heart about why your situation is unfolding as it is? Have you allowed Him to make you teachable in those difficult moments?

David misread his situation terribly and then reacted to what he thought was happening. Sound familiar? It should, because we have all done this. Our wrong thinking leads us to make bad decisions that in turn wreak havoc in our lives, and all the while the Holy Spirit is trying to get us to stop, be still, and allow Him to speak into our lives and clarify our world.

I spent three years of my life in direct disobedience to God, and yet I was in church every week, in small groups during the week, and in leadership meetings on Saturday mornings! Yet the whole time I was running from God's will. I had given the Lord an open invitation to have my life and do His will in me, but when He took the lead, I resisted Him, because His plan had no semblance to what I expected He would do. In those three years everything I touched broke, and everything I tried to build failed. It was an incredibly painful time. It was a crucial and life-shaping time, but it was ever so difficult. As it turned out, the difficulty was God trying to bend my will and turn me back home.

Maybe you are there today. Stop and be still. Ask God to speak clearly to you. His Word often speaks about Him disciplining us because of His deep love for us. Realize that the pain in your life may very well be His loving hand touching your heart. "My son, do not reject the discipline of the LORD or loathe His reproof, for whom the LORD loves He reproves, even as a father corrects the son in whom he delights" (Prov. 3:11–12). "It's the child he loves that he disciplines; the child he embraces, he also corrects" (Heb. 12:6, MSG). "Those whom I love I rebuke and discipline. So be earnest and repent" (Rev. 3:19, NIV).

PRAYER

Father, when I hear the word "discipline," I tend to think I am in deep trouble. Holy Spirit, teach me that the love of the Father holds correction for His children. Please remind me of this so that I will find freedom to run to Your arms instead of running away. Amen.

Day 48

He Is Your Glory and Shield

O Lord, how my adversaries have increased! Many are rising up against me. Many are saying of my soul, "There is no deliverance for him in God." But You, O Lord, are a shield about me, my glory, and the One who lifts my head. I was crying to the Lord with my voice, and He answered me from His holy mountain. I lay down and slept; I awoke, for the Lord sustains me. I will not be afraid of ten thousands of people who have set themselves against me round about. Arise, O Lord; save me, O my God!

Psalm 3:1–7

When David's dreams died, he did the one thing that sustained him and made him the great man he was: he ran to God. Oh, if each of us would be as wise. When pain closes in and circumstances overwhelm us, we should run not to others first but straight to the Lord. He is, as David said in Psalm 3, a shield about us, our glory and the One who lifts our heads. David wrote this psalm when his son Absalom was attempting to overthrow him and take his throne because of David's own failures as a father and king.

In times of trouble, we have two choices: we can run to God or run from Him. Often we believe that if someone has wounded us or some circumstance beyond our control has us in great difficulty, then we have liberty to bring our troubles to God, but if our problems are of our own making, then we must handle them ourselves. But when we fail to run to Jesus, we compound our difficulties by telling ourselves that we have no place with Him. We somehow believe that His love for us is built on our actions, when in reality His love for us is built on who He is, not what we do.

David understood this principle so well that even though his problems were almost entirely of his own making, he still ran to God. He still found the Lord to be his answer, because David understood grace—the life-giving grace of Jesus. God's kindness is amazing and healing. It is just as David wrote of Him who can save us: "I was crying to the LORD with my voice, and He answered me from His holy mountain. . . . The LORD sustains me. . . . Arise, O LORD; save me, O my God!"

Jesus is here today to save you. Cry out to Him as David did, and ask the Holy Spirit to convince you today that Jesus is your answer, no matter what your problem is. Ask Him to teach you in your innermost being that His love and grace toward you are not bound up in what you do but in who He is.

PRAYER

Holy Spirit, today I ask You to convince me of how deeply I am loved by Jesus. Teach me of His heart of love toward me and how His grace can heal my heart and all my broken situations. Thank You, Lord, that Your love toward me isn't built on what I do but on who You are. Amen.

Day 49

Don't Give Up, Give Thanks

Do not be anxious about anything, but in every situation, by prayer and petition, with thanksgiving, present your requests to God. And the peace of God, which transcends all understanding, will guard your hearts and your minds in Christ Jesus.

Philippians 4:6–7, NIV

When life comes at us in waves and we feel like we are going to be washed away, prayer is always the wisest choice. Prayer connects our hearts to heaven in a way that provides hope in the midst of despair, healing in the midst of deep pain, and promise when we feel abandoned.

But prayer actually does something more when it is combined with thanks. When we give thanks, or offer thanksgiving, our perspective is altered, our hard hearts are softened, and we see things as God sees them. Paul said, "In everything with thanksgiving pray." "Everything" is a huge, all-inclusive word. In small things that nag us, in big things that wreck us, in everything that happens in our lives, God has the possibility to move if we will invite Him into our circumstances. Praying with thanksgiving does exactly that. It opens the windows of heaven because we are no longer kicking and screaming but rather thanking God for things we still don't understand, things we often would rather not encounter, and things we wish would go away but won't.

When we stop and actually thank God, our perspective enlarges from our selfish little outlooks to eternal ones. We begin to see that God is still for us and that these things that threaten us might actually be the answer to prayers we have prayed to grow, to become larger inside, to be more patient and kind and loving toward others. Yes, thanksgiving can do all this—it is a powerful tool in God's arsenal.

It is too easy to lose our way when things go south, to turn on God and, without even realizing it, shut Him out. Thanksgiving reopens those doors. "Give thanks to the LORD, for he is good; his love endures forever. . . . Let them give thanks to the LORD for his unfailing love and his wonderful deeds for mankind, for he satisfies the thirsty and fills the hungry with good things" (Ps. 107:1–9, NIV).

Give thanks when you want to give up. Give thanks when you feel ungrateful. Give thanks "to the LORD, for he is good; his love endures forever." Remember, no matter how bad life feels, God is still good. Turn to Him, run to Him, and open up your heart to Him with thanksgiving, and He will move in your midst.

PRAYER

Father, so often when life crashes into me, I flee from You, the One I should run to, and run to my own resources and possibilities. But when I do this, things only get worse. I want to grow in thanksgiving when life is hard. Teach me to run to You with a heart that is grateful for a God who will never leave me and whose love endures no matter what I do. Amen.

Day 50

Praise and Thanks

Rejoice always; pray without ceasing; in everything give thanks; for this is God's will for you in Christ Jesus.

1 Thessalonians 5:16–18

Praise, prayer, and thanksgiving go together. They are often found in close company. Praise and thanksgiving are often outward and verbal, while prayer is often quiet and inward, but they are found together over and over in the Bible. Thanksgiving and praise are the results of prayer. Gratitude arises when we pray and our eyes move off our small world of trials and troubles and into God's world of eternal perspective. When this happens, gratitude grows deep inside us, and thanksgiving is the outward expression of it. We give thanks to God for moving in and around us. This gives rise to praise, an outward declaration of God's greatness and His mercy.

Psalm 116 puts it this way:

> I love the LORD, because He hears My voice and my supplications. Because He has inclined His ear to me, therefore I shall call upon Him as long as I live. . . . To You I shall offer a sacrifice of thanksgiving, and call upon the name of the LORD. I shall pay my vows to the LORD, oh may it be in the presence of all His people, in the courts of the LORD's house, in the midst of you, O Jerusalem. Praise the LORD! (Ps. 116:1–19)

This psalm is clearly about prayer and gratitude, covered in thanksgiving, bursting forth with praise that changes our perspective. When we give ourselves to prayer, we reap many benefits, but one of the greatest is a fresh perspective. Prayer gives us a new perspective on our old problems. When we bring our struggles to the Lord and lay them out before Him, the Holy Spirit does something amazing: without minimizing our plights, He alters our perspectives by reminding us, as badly as we might feel or think things are, that our problems are still small in light of eternity. He reminds us that He has saved us and healed us and that He will save us again from whatever it is that afflicts us now. His peace flows in our direction, and our hearts begin to rise up with thanksgiving. It doesn't take long for that to turn into praise and adoration for the great and amazing power God releases toward us and our issues.

Paul taught the same thing in Colossians 4:2, where he wrote, "Devote yourselves to prayer, keeping alert in it with an attitude of thanksgiving." When you are down, and things just feel impossible, don't quit. Run to Jesus, lay your circumstances out before Him, and as He enters into your situation, begin to praise Him and thank Him for His wonderful and powerful ability to set things straight.

PRAYER

Father, prayer, praise, and thanksgiving are so much better than my grumbling spirit. Please, Holy Spirit, teach me to come to You every day for Your eternal perspective on my journey. Amen.

Day 51

In the Lion's Den

The king gave orders for Daniel to be arrested and thrown into the den of lions. The king said to him, "May your God, whom you serve so faithfully, rescue you."

Daniel 6:16, NLT

We have all at one time or another cried out to God and asked Him to rescue us. We may have needed to be rescued from a mess we had gotten ourselves into or a situation that overpowered us and swept us away. Daniel faced a similar situation. His enemies had set a trap for him. He was fully aware of it, yet he willingly walked into it, because he believed that his God was greater than the men's trap. He knew whom he loved, and he knew that God had his life in His hand.

When we are in crisis, knowing that we are in God's hand is crucial to our ability not only to survive the situation but also to thrive in the journey. Daniel was in one crisis after another, yet he was steadfast, immovable, always abounding in the Lord. He was the man Jesus described in Matthew 7:24–27:

> Anyone who listens to my teaching and follows it is wise, like a person who builds a house on solid rock. Though the rain comes in torrents and the floodwaters rise and the winds beat against that house, it won't collapse because it is built on bedrock. But anyone who hears my teaching and doesn't obey it is foolish, like a person who builds a

> house on sand. When the rains and floods come and the winds beat against that house, it will collapse with a mighty crash. (NLT)

What are you building your house on—the wisdom and words of men or the Word of God? Are you building on the power and authority you have gleaned in this world or the touch of the Holy Spirit? The storms will come, and for some of us, like Daniel, it seems that our whole lives are one crisis after another. When the storms come, will your life stand? Is your life built on the rock of Jesus or the words of men?

When the king came to check on Daniel the morning after Daniel had been thrown into the lion's den, he made an astounding statement: "Daniel, servant of the living God! Was your God, whom you serve so faithfully, able to rescue you from the lions?" (Dan. 6:20, NLT). "The living God" is an apt description of our God and one that is used over and over in the Bible. We serve the living God, not an idol or a statue but the living God who hears our cries and watches our journeys. He is our rescuer!

In the storm, in the crisis, remember what Daniel knew: we serve a living God who is able to rescue us! Run to Him, cry out to Him, and expect Him to help you, and He will. Trust Him, and He will come to your aid. He is always faithful to those who seek Him.

PRAYER

Father, in the crisis remind me that You alone are the living God. There is nowhere else to go but to You. You are my rescue. Teach me to come to You daily and to build my house on You, Jesus, so that when the storms come, I will be steadfast. Amen.

Day 52

God Delights in You!

He brought me forth also into a broad place; He rescued me, because He delighted in me.

Psalm 18:19

Time and time again David found himself tested and tried. His life often seemed to be one huge crisis. Yet in the midst of all the drama, David grew. He grew strong enough not only to survive his struggles but also to thrive in the midst of them. Here in Psalm 18 David was being pursued by King Saul, who wanted to track him down and kill him. Yet David opened the psalm with praise!

> "I love You, O Lord, my strength." The Lord is my rock and my fortress and my deliverer, my God, my rock, in whom I take refuge; my shield and the horn of my salvation, my stronghold. I call upon the Lord, who is worthy to be praised, and I am saved from my enemies. (Ps. 18:1–3)

Praise is our answer in times of trouble. Praise breaks unbelief, and it releases the power and presence of God into our situations. Praise, though, is often hard to come by when we are first struck with news of a crisis. Our first response is often defensive: "How can I protect myself?" But when we react this way, we are immediately closing off our single greatest resource in the time of need: God.

David learned important lessons during his times of testing, lessons we all need to learn: that God is our rock, our fortress, and our deliverer. We cannot deliver ourselves, but we have a great resource who is a stronghold and place of safety and who is worthy to be praised in both our tough times and our times of plenty.

Praise enlarges our hearts and allows us to embrace God when we would prefer to run. Praise alters our circumstances because it embraces God's presence and possibilities in spite of our tests or needs. When David declared, "He brought me out into this spacious or broad place," we see that his praise had enlarged his situation to include his God. What else could this broad or spacious place be but his God!

When testing comes, don't cower and believe the lie that your God has abandoned you. No! He is your ever-present help in time of need. He is your help when you feel helpless. Hell wants you to buy the lie that God doesn't care for you and that's why you're in a tough situation, but nothing could be further from the truth. Look at David's words in the midst of his battle: "He rescued me, because He delighted in me." David settled this most important issue that God was for him and had rescued him because He was crazy about him. That one critical belief allowed David to open up in praise in the middle of crisis. He knew God delighted in him.

God delights in you and me as well, and His heart for us opens to each of us this huge vista of praise that will engulf us and rescue us in our times of need.

PRAYER

Father, thank You for delighting in me! What an amazing thought. Teach me to run to You and praise You in times of need, knowing that You will rescue me because You delight in me. Amen.

Day 53

Confidence in God

Our enemies found out that I had finished rebuilding the wall and that no gaps remained—though we had not yet set up the doors in the gates. So Sanballat and Geshem sent a message asking me to meet them at one of the villages in the plain of Ono. But I realized they were plotting to harm me.

Nehemiah 6:1–2, NLT

We have all been threatened. Sometimes the threat is minor, and sometimes, as in the case with Nehemiah, it is huge. Threats cause many different reactions in us: fear rises up, our walls go up, our defenses take over. These responses are certainly good if we are facing a real and dangerous threat, but they can be bad if they are sent by the enemy with only one purpose in mind: to paralyze our faith and cause us to lose our way.

First Peter 5:8 reminds us, "Stay alert! Watch out for your great enemy, the devil. He prowls around like a roaring lion, looking for someone to devour" (NLT). Satan wants to intimidate us into silence. He does this by threatening us as he did Nehemiah. His goal is to stop us in our tracks and keep us from our Father's heart. If we allow our fears to move unchecked, they will crush our faith. Faith and fear cannot coexist. That is why it is crucial when we feel threatened that we run to our refuge, Jesus.

David, like Nehemiah, faced threats. In fact, when King Saul chased David, his threat was not only real but also active. Yet look at David's response to his fear:

> The LORD is my light and my salvation—whom shall I fear? The LORD is the stronghold of my life—of whom shall I be afraid?
>
> When the wicked advance against me to devour me, it is my enemies and my foes who will stumble and fall. Though an army besiege me, my heart will not fear; though war break out against me, even then I will be confident. . . .
>
> Hear my voice when I call, LORD; be merciful to me and answer me. My heart says of you, "Seek his face!" Your face, LORD, I will seek. (Ps. 27:1–8, NIV)

David had a confidence in his God that created a shield about him. It is this kind of confidence that the Holy Spirit wants to place in you today—that no matter what or who comes against you, no matter how fear attacks you, your confidence and safety will not be shaken. When your heart says, "Seek His face," then run to Him, and do not fear, for the battle is His, not yours.

PRAYER

Father, teach me to seek Your face, to find You to be a shelter from my fears. Set me on Your rock so I won't be threatened by the roar of the enemy. "God is our refuge and strength, a very present help in trouble. Therefore we will not fear, though the earth should change and though the mountains slip into the heart of the sea; though its waters roar and foam, though the mountains quake at its swelling pride" (Ps. 46:1–3). Amen.

Day 54

Faith over Fear

All of them were trying to frighten us, thinking, "They will become discouraged with the work and it will not be done." But now, O God, strengthen my hands. . . . So the wall was completed on the twenty-fifth of the month Elul, in fifty-two days. When all our enemies heard of it, and all the nations surrounding us saw it, they lost their confidence; for they recognized that this work had been accomplished with the help of our God.

Nehemiah 6:9–16

When Nehemiah first came to Jerusalem, he found a battered and bruised people, a people who lived in fear and had little faith. The embarrassing evidence was their city that lay in shambles. The people were defenseless and at the mercy of their enemies. They were unable to recover from the ruins of their past, because their fears held them captive. Many of us today are in similar situations. When we become frightened by challenges, it is easy to lose our way and give into fears that long ago should have been healed in us. When this happens, we become discouraged and give up. We surrender not to the Spirit but to our flesh and to the plan of the enemy.

Nehemiah brought his faith to the Jews. He prayed often, and he believed God to enter into this situation with power that would overcome his fears and allow him to be used as a tool to bring life to these wandering hearts in Jerusalem. This positioned Nehemiah to bring Jesus' life to them. He was tender, kind, and understanding. He was patient. Above all, he was persistent!

Nehemiah's determination led the people to life. He taught them to pray, to live in the Word and resist their adversary, to battle against the attacks of the enemy. He taught them to care for each other and serve each other. He built confidence in them that together they could accomplish more than they had ever dreamed—and they did! He allowed the Spirit of the Lord to redeem and restore them as a people. Nehemiah's confidence in the strength of the Lord allowed these captive people to break free from fear and release faith and life in their community. This is what Jesus wants to do in us today!

When we are challenged to believe for our healing, it is easy for us to say, "It will never happen," and if that's how we choose to think, we will be correct. You see, our unbelief blocks God's work in us. We may think that our self-assessment is humble, but our sense that somehow we are above God healing us is in fact prideful. Stop and humble your heart before our magnificent King and remember this saying: "Today is the day; you are the person. You make the choice; God will make the change. Without us God won't, and without Him we can't!"

Yield to God today. Just say yes, and watch His strong hand strengthen you and His Spirit's touch heal you as He did Nehemiah and the people of Jerusalem.

PRAYER

Father, today I humble my heart and ask You to forgive me for my unbelief. Strengthen me as You did Nehemiah, and use me to touch and heal those around me. Amen.

DAY 55

Trust in God

*Do not fear, for I am with you; do not anxiously look about you,
for I am your God. I will strengthen you, surely I will help you,
surely I will uphold you with My righteous right hand.*

ISAIAH 41:10

When we are afraid, we should always ask ourselves one question: "Can God be trusted?" This is a huge life question that we all have to face. If we can settle it, we can face our fears head on and win the battle over them. If God can be trusted, then most certainly we should trust Him! We know that He's crazy about us, that He loves us, that He is a shield about us, that He is our protector and Father. But can He be trusted?

Isaiah believed He could be. God spoke through the prophet Isaiah about fear, declaring, "Do not fear, for I am with you." The Lord's statement is all about trust. Can we count on God? Will He show up? God has one answer: "I am with you." We can trust God with our fears, because He is with us; He will remain with us no matter what we face. His presence in our circumstance gives us the power and possibility to remain safe and calm. In the battle the one thing God promised to Israel was His presence (see Deut. 31:6–8). In our battles He has promised us the same power to enable us to keep faith and hold off fear: His presence. His presence is a promise, today and every day. The writer of Hebrews reminds us that we have this guarantee: "I will never desert you, nor will I ever forsake you." That is why we can confidently say, "The Lord is my helper, I will not be afraid. What will man do to me?"(Heb. 13:5–6).

"Do not fear, . . . do not anxiously look about you," Isaiah wrote. It is so human for us to quickly look around for help when we are afraid. We learned to do this as children, and most of us carry the habit into adulthood. But God says, "Don't anxiously look about you. Look to Me, for I am your God, and I am here."

Isaiah 41 gives us five promises that should help protect us from fear:

- "I am with you"
- "I am your God"
- "I will strengthen you"
- "I will help you"
- "I will uphold you with my hand"

God hungers to care for His kids. His great desire is for each of us to run to Him in times of trouble, to find our safety and security in His presence, to know Him and His character. He gives us His Word, and He keeps His Word. If He promises to be with us and strengthen us and help us and uphold us, then we have just one job: to believe that He is our God! He will do the rest.

PRAYER

Father, today I declare that my trust is in You! It is Your presence in my circumstances that will protect and guard me. Thank You for always keeping Your promises to me. Amen.

Day 56

Friendship and Obedience

The secret of the LORD is for those who fear Him,
and He will make them know His covenant.

Psalm 25:14

Of all the people we read about in the Bible, none had intimacy with God like David. He was the ultimate worshiper. He unlocked the secret of intimacy with God. He wrote and wrote of his love for God and God's love for him. He often said that he delighted in God and that God delighted in him.

For those of us who long for more of God, it's easy to read about David and go away discouraged, feeling as if David lived at a level with God that none of us could ever reach. But that is a huge mistake. David wrote of his love for God because he desired others to find the same deep intimacy with God that he had. He saw closeness with God as a treasure that could be found by those hungry enough to search with their whole hearts.

When David wrote, "The secret of the LORD is for those who fear Him," he was saying just that. The word "secret" is about intimacy with God; it literally means God's "counsel" or "purposes." God shares His secrets, or His purposes, with those who fear Him. But the end of that statement trips many of us up today—"fear Him." We have been taught that to fear is bad or indicates distance from God. But David ties fearing God to friendship and intimacy with Him. It means to honor, respect, or obey God.

Jesus spoke of this in John 14:15 when He gave direction to His disciples on His last night on Earth: "If you love Me, you will keep My commandments." He went on in verses 23–24, "Anyone who loves me will obey my teaching. My Father will love them, and we will come to them and make our home with them. Anyone who does not love me will not obey my teaching" (NIV). Jesus tied obeying and intimacy together: if we love Him, we obey Him; if we don't love Him, we don't obey Him. It's very simple but deeply profound.

David wanted us to understand that God longs to impart His heart, His deepest thoughts, to us, but He will do that only with those He can trust—those who obey Him and His directions. The noun translated as "secret" can also be translated as "friendship." We tell our secrets to those closest to us, our friends, and our Father is no different. When Jesus talked about friendship with us, He tied it directly to our obeying Him: "You are My friends if you do what I command you" (John 15:14).

Learning to say yes to God every day in every situation will build intimacy between you and your Father. This may seem like a tall order, but it is within your reach. It is relationship, friendship, with God. Taking the time to feel His heart and obey His voice will unlock His secrets and His friendship to you.

PRAYER

Father, when I think about obeying, I can quickly feel overwhelmed and believe that it is impossible. But, Holy Spirit, please remind me that with You living inside me, nothing is impossible, including friendship with God. Amen.

Day 57

Fix Your Eyes on God

We don't look at the troubles we can see now; rather, we fix our gaze on things that cannot be seen. For the things we see now will soon be gone, but the things we cannot see will last forever.

2 Corinthians 4:18, NLT

We live in a day when the world is overwhelmed with troubles. Maybe it's always been this way, but it has likely never felt so overwhelming until the last generation of technology created a worldwide pipeline that feeds us a daily dose of all that is wrong with our troubled world. Just a few moments on our phones or tablets in the morning are enough to shipwreck a day. But why look at the troubles around us? Why fix our gaze on them? I am not advocating being a recluse or hiding in the mountains as some sort of survivalist. I am suggesting that dwelling on the deep and troubling issues that our world offers us daily as news will not bring us life.

Paul suggests that we instead "fix our gaze on things that cannot be seen." This word "gaze," or "look," is *skope* in the original language. It means to ponder, to let one's mind dwell on, to keep thinking about, to fix one's attention on. It can also mean to turn our interests or expectations toward something and respond accordingly. When we *skopeo* the news, we see the troubles of our day, and we set our minds and hearts on things that will soon be gone. Our interests and expectations shift from being godly to being troubled and worldly. We get stuck responding to things that will perish. Yes, this is the world we live in today, but Paul suggests that we look at the things unseen by most people—spiritual things, supernatural things, godly things.

We are told not to fix our eyes on this world but on the next one. We are not to get caught up in the web of discouragement the nightly news can bring but to believe beyond what we see and hear and read. When we gaze on God's Word and His promises, we gain His perspective on this life and on our world's troubles. He gives us His eternal point of view that will allow us to see the news but not lose our hearts.

Each day determine not to fix your eyes or your hope on the daily news but on Jesus: "Let us fix our eyes on Jesus, the pioneer and perfecter of our faith, who for the joy set before Him endured the cross, scorning its shame, and sat down at the right hand of the throne of God" (Heb. 12:2, BSB). Fix your eyes on Jesus, the One who builds our faith as we keep our eyes on Him. He will keep your heart and your head clear. In Him you will find hope in the troubles of this hurting world.

PRAYER

Father, forgive me for allowing the news to overwhelm my spirit. Teach me, Holy Spirit, that each day belongs to You and that You are working out Your will and Your way in our troubled world. As I fix my eyes on You, Jesus, build my faith today. Amen.

Day 58

Acting According to Faith

He was hired for this reason, that I might become frightened and act accordingly and sin, so that they might have an evil report in order that they could reproach me.

Nehemiah 6:13

Fear is incredibly powerful. It can override every other emotion. It can pierce the heart and choke the spirit. Franklin D. Roosevelt's famous word to the Americans entering into World War II was extremely accurate: "The only thing we have to fear is fear itself."

Fear is Satan's greatest asset. That is why Jesus cautioned us about our fears. When Jesus was asleep in a boat crossing the Sea of Galilee, a huge storm arose, and with it a huge amount of fear overtook the disciples. When they woke Jesus from His nap, they exclaimed, "Save us, Lord; we are perishing!" Jesus' response to them should help us realize how damaging our fears can be: "Why are you afraid, you men of little faith?" (Matt. 8:25–26).

Our fears and our faith are inextricably tied together. When fear takes over, we do as Nehemiah wrote: we "act accordingly and sin." We lose faith, and with it we lose courage and perspective.

Jesus taught against fear over and over again. He spent time encouraging people and then told them, "Do not fear," or, "Don't be afraid." In Luke 12:4 Jesus made an amazingly eternal statement about what really counts when He said, "Dear friends, don't be afraid of those who want to kill your body; they cannot do any more to you after that" (NLT). Don't be afraid of them—all they can do is kill you! Wow, what a thought. Dying is exactly what many of us are afraid of, isn't it? But life doesn't end for us when we no longer exist on this planet; life is eternal. Jesus went on to say, "So don't be afraid, little flock. For it gives your Father great happiness to give you the Kingdom" (Luke 12:32, NLT).

The kingdom is eternal. Our lives as believers are eternal. It's all about perspective, isn't it? Fear causes us to lose God's perspective, and then we "act accordingly and sin." We do things we should never do and say things we should never say.

In order to get the eternal perspective Jesus has, we have to spend time with Him. We need our thinking changed, and when that happens, our hearts change, and we "act accordingly" without fear. When we worship and yield to the Holy Spirit, He breaks our bondage to fear and releases faith. Peter's early years with Jesus were often marked by his fears, yet as he grew in the Lord, an amazing deliverance took place that allowed him to walk with Jesus' eternal perspective and without fear. He fell into the healing grace of God and then lived his life out of that grace. "The God of all grace, who called you to his eternal glory in Christ, after you have suffered a little while, will himself restore you and make you strong, firm and steadfast" (1 Pet. 5:10, NIV).

PRAYER

Father, when I give in to my fears, I "act accordingly and sin." Forgive me, and draw me near to You. Holy Spirit, heal me of my deep-seated fears, and release new life and faith in me today. Amen.

Day 59

A Gentle Word Can Save the Day

When Abigail saw David, she hurried and dismounted from her donkey, and fell on her face before David and bowed herself to the ground. She fell at his feet and said, "On me alone, my lord, be the blame. And please let your maidservant speak to you, and listen to the words of your maidservant." . . . Then David said to Abigail, "Blessed be the L*ORD God of Israel, who sent you this day to meet me, and blessed be your discernment, and blessed be you, who have kept me this day from bloodshed and from avenging myself by my own hand."*

1 SAMUEL 25:23–33

This wild story in 1 Samuel 25 is about a wise woman whose husband had greatly offended David, and when she heard about it, she made the issue hers to reconcile.

God has offered us wisdom that goes miles when we end up in heated situations: "A gentle answer turns away wrath, but a harsh word stirs up anger" (Prov. 15:1). The New Living Translation puts it this way: "A gentle answer deflects anger, but harsh words make tempers flare." When we are offended, a gentle word is generally the furthest thing from our minds. But when the Holy Spirit begins to speak to us in times of conflict, He will always remind us, "A gentle word heals, but a harsh response makes it all worse."

I remember the day the Lord taught me this lesson. A bunch of us guys were playing Frisbee golf in the street, and a guy's Frisbee hit a car parked in the street. It didn't dent or scratch the car, but the owner came flying out of his garage and lit into the guy. I was a young Christian and a six-foot-eight college basketball player, and I was in no mood for this guy to cuss my buddy out. I started to move in on the guy when my friend said, "No, stop, he's right. I was completely wrong for not being more thoughtful about his car. I'm very sorry." The owner of the car, like me, didn't know what to do. He was totally disarmed, and my friends and I picked up our Frisbees and went on our way. Later my friend quoted Proverbs 15:1 to me and told me it was the Holy Spirit who had empowered the scripture in the man's heart and softened his attitude. I was astounded. All I knew was to ramp things up and make them worse, but Jesus had a better way.

Nabal, the man who had offended David, lived up to his name (it means "a fool" or "to be foolish"). But Abigail's humble, kind, and gentle response saved David from making a tragic mistake. When things get intense and hard, stop, bow your heart, and ask for supernatural power to speak kindly into others' lives. Jesus will give it to you.

PRAYER

Jesus, my whole life I have been taught to respond to others' anger with anger. Teach me, Lord, that a gentle word turns away anger and that You, Holy Spirit, can help me respond to injustice against me with kindness. I want You to have Your way in me, so please move in me today. Amen.

Day 60

Rest in the Lord

The fourth beast will be a fourth kingdom on the earth, which will be different from all the other kingdoms and will devour the whole earth and tread it down and crush it. . . . [A king] will speak out against the Most High and wear down the saints of the Highest One, and he will intend to make alterations in times and in law; and they will be given into his hand for a time, times, and half a time.

Daniel 7:23–25

Life has a way of making us all tired at one time or another. Frustrations, stress, emotions, and schedules can wear us down if we don't learn to live with some margin. There is a spiritual side to tiredness as well. When we are tired, our defenses are down, our discernment is low, and our emotions can get high. Tiredness makes us vulnerable to giving in to things we would otherwise stand against. Daniel 7:23–25 makes it clear that the enemy has strategies that he will use at the end of time to destroy people, and one of those is to "wear down the saints of the Highest One."

The Hebrew word for "wear down" literally means "to wear away" or "to wear out" as one would wear out a garment. This tactic of slowly rubbing believers wrong is not something Satan will suddenly come up with at the end of time. He is actually quite good at it right now—getting us busy and keeping us irritated so we slowly but surely wear down and lower our defenses, allowing him to get us into a place where we are neither wise nor godly. Tiredness can be dangerous for us if we live there too long.

This is one of the reasons the Bible speaks often of the need for us to rest. Psalm 37:7 says, "Rest in the LORD and wait patiently for Him; do not fret because of him who prospers in his way, because of the man who carries out wicked schemes." Jesus put it this way: "Come to me, all of you who are weary and carry heavy burdens, and I will give you rest. Take my yoke upon you. Let me teach you, because I am humble and gentle at heart, and you will find rest for your souls. For my yoke is easy to bear, and the burden I give you is light" (Matt. 11:28–30).

Rest is crucial if we are going to flourish in Jesus. We would do well to realize that rest is actually a form of spiritual warfare. Rest keeps the enemy from wearing us down and making us vulnerable. It allows for stillness in our souls and spirits that then allows the Holy Spirit to work deeply in us. Sure, we will go through times of busyness and even weariness. Those are part of life. But we would be wise to keep them fewer and further apart, allowing rest to come and pour out freshness from the Spirit on us. Then we will be strong and alert, in a better place to withstand the attacks of the enemy.

PRAYER

Father, I am guilty of doing too much far too often. Please teach me that limits and margins are not weakness but wisdom. Holy Spirit, I ask You to come and refresh me as I stop to rest in You today. Amen.

Days 61–90

Impacting the World Through Powerful Prayer

Do we have any idea of the power God has
put in our midst through prayer?
We are called to make a difference in our world,
and it cannot be done without prayer—
earnest prayer.

Day 61

The Gift of Friendship

Daniel, Hananiah, Mishael, and Azariah were four of the young men chosen, all from the tribe of Judah.

DANIEL 1:6

While Daniel was in captivity, he had something Joseph never did: friends. Daniel had friends to grow with, go through the tests with, pray with (see Dan. 1:3–20; 2:17–18). He had friends who spoke his language and knew the world he had grown up in. Friends make all the difference in the world—people in our lives whom we can count on, who are strong in faith, who are able to stand with us when we are weak, who bring a word of encouragement at just the right time. Daniel's faith and the faith of his friends would be deeply tested by their captivity, but together they would stand. Together they could thrive.

Friendship is an exciting and thrilling thing when God is in it. When He weaves our hearts into another person's and vice versa, we feel as though we have known that person all our lives, even when we may have met him or her just a few months or years ago. The word "friend" in the New Testament has many different connotations, but one that is found everywhere is a picture of what I like to call familiarness. It describes well what a friend is—one who is familiar with us, close to us, beloved and dear to us.

Jesus spoke of friendship His last night on Earth. He said,

> There is no greater love than to lay down one's life for one's friends. You are my friends if you do what I command. I no longer call you slaves, because a master doesn't confide in his slaves. Now you are my friends, since I have told you everything the Father told me. (John 15:13–15, NLT)

Jesus' friendship penetrates deep into our souls and spirits. He takes the time to become familiar with us—our fears and joys, our failures and successes, our dreams and despair. His Spirit is ever probing us to create deeper intimacy that is born out of our knowing Him and His knowing us. Friendship with Jesus is a huge part of really knowing Him.

Friendship doesn't mean taking advantage of someone but trusting and honoring him or her. Jesus said that we are His friends when we obey Him. When we are intimate with Him and His Spirit directs us and we respond to Him not as slaves but as friends, intimacy and friendship grow. We are happy to please Him and do as He asks, because He is our friend with whom we share affection and trust. When we walk with Him, He speaks to us. He confides in us, and intimacy can flourish.

PRAYER

Jesus, today I want my friendship with You to flourish. I want to walk intimately with You, and I want You to speak life and hope into me. Remove my fear, and fill me with faith to trust that You are my friend. Amen.

Day 62

Relationship with Your Father

This, then, is how you should pray: "Our Father in heaven, hallowed be your name."

Matthew 6:9, NIV

The idea that God is "our Father" is one that most Jews could hardly entertain. It was amazing to them that God, their God who was so great, so mighty, and the Creator of the heavens and the earth, would dare to be called their Father. Yet that is exactly what Jesus said to call God when His disciples asked Him to teach them to pray. He said to pray like this: "Our Father." Later Jesus took this idea to another level by calling God an Arabic word, *Abba*, which for us translates as "Daddy." This word removes the authority aspect and replaces it with relationship. Relationship with our heavenly Dad is undoubtedly what Jesus had in mind when He first suggested that His followers pray "Our Father." This relationship was to be nurtured and to grow in prayer.

Relationships are born out of trust. But trust in God only comes when we know who we are praying to: our Father! Effective prayer is a partnership, and we cannot partner with a stranger—it takes relationship. Many of us have a hard time with prayer because we have a hard time imagining that God, as great as He is, could love us. It's what I call the "love issue." It overwhelms many of us and not in a good way. We are convinced, wrongly, that God couldn't possibly love us since He is as great as He is and we are, well, just so human. But Jesus made it clear that our Father wants relationship with us. All Jesus' life was spent building relationships with those He loved, and the book of Hebrews tells us, "The Son is the radiance of God's glory and the exact representation of his being" (Heb. 1:3, NIV).

Who do you pray to? This God who is crazy about you and controls the universe, who gave His Son to save your life? Or someone else?

If God is your Father, you should not pray like an orphan instead of a son or daughter. Enjoy your Father. Come into His presence with a thankful heart. You don't have to beg Him for life. He wants to bless you. Believe in His abundance; believe that He is a giver. He wants to give you abundant life, so begging isn't necessary; begging comes with a poverty mentality. Jesus often asked those in need, "What do you want Me to do for you? What do you want Me to restore and heal?" He is asking you the same thing. Run to your Father today, and know that His arms are open wide to you!

PRAYER

Jesus, please teach me to see You as completely representing my Father's heart. Holy Spirit, lead me into intimacy with God. Remove my fear, and replace it with life and an excitement to know my Father better. Amen.

Day 63

Prioritizing God's Presence

One thing I ask from the LORD, this only do I seek: that I may dwell in the house of the LORD all the days of my life, to gaze on the beauty of the LORD and to seek him in his temple.

PSALM 27:4, NIV

Most of us learned early on as children that if we needed something, we asked our parents. It was their responsibility to care for us and provide for us. Most of us never even considered whether or not they should or shouldn't do this; we just knew they did. We had parents, and they took care of us, and thankfully for most of us, they did. Some of us learned to ask by screaming or crying. A few of us actually learned to say "please." We never considered whether asking was good or bad; we just did it.

The same is true in our relationship with God. Asking is the law of the kingdom, and we see this in every story of every leader we read in the Bible. They learned this lesson early and well. David is no exception. He knew that the key to touching his Father's heart was dependence on Him, and he knew that dependence was tied to asking—asking in prayer for what he needed and wanted.

Here in Psalm 27:4 David makes a big request. He said that he really wanted only one thing, and if he could have that one thing, all else would be well: "That I may dwell in the house of the LORD all the days of my life, to gaze on the beauty of the LORD and to seek him in his temple." What an incredible thing to ask! To be in the presence of God, to dwell with Him, to experience His majesty and splendor; David believed this would make all else well.

What if we thought like that? What if our priority was God's presence every day? What if we understood that if we made our way into the Lord's presence each day through prayer and worship, praise and adoration, then all else would be well? All our depression, discouragement, failures, and successes would balance out under His presence.

It is not our responsibility to carry the weight of the world on our shoulders. It is God's place to lift our burdens and lighten our loads; it is our place to seek God's face and to worship ourselves into the Lord's presence. In God's presence is fullness of joy, hope and life, healing and possibility. Make it your heart's desire and the object of your prayers to dwell in the house of the Lord all the days of your life.

PRAYER

Father, give me a heart like David's that seeks after Your heart, not only in crisis but every day. Holy Spirit, teach me to worship You and find my way into the Father's presence. Amen.

Day 64

The Favor of God

God had given the chief of staff both respect and affection for Daniel. . . . Whenever the king consulted [Daniel and his three friends] in any matter requiring wisdom and balanced judgment, he found them ten times more capable than any of the magicians and enchanters in his entire kingdom.

Daniel 1:9–20

Daniel had the favor of God on his life. Clearly he was esteemed beyond others. Doors opened for him that remained shut to many others. It would be easy for us to think he had earned this favor, but if we did, we would miss the gracious hand of God in his circumstances.

To favor means "to give special regard to; to treat with goodwill; to show exceptional kindness to someone."[1] Sometimes it means to show extra kindness in comparison to the treatment of others or preferential treatment, though biblical favor is not always used this way. It sometimes simply means that the one favored is shown kindness and treated with a generosity and goodwill far beyond what would normally be expected. This is generally the favor we receive from Jesus. We are treated much better than we could expect.

God gives favor to those who seek Him. This is found all over in the Bible, from Moses with Pharaoh, to Nehemiah with King Artaxerxes, to Paul with King Agrippa. God opens doors for those who serve and seek Him:

> The boy Samuel was growing in stature and in favor both with the LORD and with men. (1 Sam. 2:26)

> Jesus kept increasing in wisdom and stature, and in favor with God and men. (Luke 2:52)

God gives favor to His people, yet we often miss His hand extending it to us. We mistakenly believe that it is our warm demeanor or wise response that has achieved favor for us, but the truth is, it is God's hand and His alone that favors us. If we stop and look back, we will be able to see that His hand has favored us. He has helped us when we didn't deserve it, opened doors that were shut to us, and made a way for us when there was no way.

Jesus gives us favor at work, at home, in circumstances we don't deserve to succeed in, because He so kindly and graciously extends it to us when we chase after Him. He gives favor in the most unlikely places—when we are out shopping and can't find what we need and suddenly a person shows up who makes it all work; in appointments that are difficult and painful and suddenly the right words flow out and healing begins to take place; in employment situations when our boss seems to notice our efforts when he or she never did before. Favor is part of the great journey with Jesus. Today ask for and watch closely for God's favor to touch your life and your journey.

PRAYER

Father, You are amazing! You favor those of us who deserve nothing, not one single thing, yet You extend grace and truth toward us. You bring healing and hope to us, and You insert Yourself into our daily situations, giving us favor. Please give me eyes to see and ears to hear when Your favor moves in my life. Amen.

Day 65

God Hears Us

This is the confidence we have in approaching God: that if we ask anything according to his will, he hears us. And if we know that he hears us—whatever we ask—we know that we have what we asked of him.

1 John 5:14-15, NIV

Confidence is an interesting thing. Sometimes when we have it, we don't realize it, but when we lose it, we certainly know it's gone. Confidence consists of faith, trust, and conviction. When we lose those things, we find ourselves on the outside looking in. Nowhere is this truer than in prayer. When we have confidence in approaching God, we have a sense of certainty, a feeling that we know He is listening and that He cares. When we lose confidence, we lose certainty. We stop coming freely, and prayer becomes a huge labor.

Jesus was always teaching about the certainty we have of the Father's love, His forgiveness, His desire to help us and be in our journeys, His promise never to leave us, His assurance that we can come to Him with confidence. Look closely at the times when Jesus prayed—He always prayed with confidence in the truth that His Father loved Him and would enter into His prayer.

Often I lack that confidence, and I have to stop and reset my heart. I have to read God's promises and allow His Spirit to speak His Word afresh into my journey. I have to clear out the cobwebs of uncertainty that have taken hold of my heart and sort out how I allowed them to grow in the first place. When I do that, confidence rises, hope takes wings, and life begins to work again. This is especially true when it concerns coming to the Father in prayer, believing that He will be there and speak into my situation.

When we are in need, we are to approach God with confidence, asking for His guidance and His way in our journeys. We are told that He hears us. That is an amazing thought. God is listening to us when we come. He is hearing us; the cries of our hearts matter! And if we know that He hears us, whatever we ask—big, small, important, or even mundane—that builds confidence in us. If we know that He hears us and that we have what we ask of Him, a certainty rises up in us that breeds hope. Then we wait on Him and watch how He responds and how His answer unfolds in our journeys.

PRAYER

Father, forgive me for not believing that You care. Some days I just lack confidence. Holy Spirit, please fill me with trust in You. I know that You are trustworthy and able to do exceedingly beyond what I could ask or think. Flood my life today with the confidence that Your Word and Your Spirit bring to living. Amen.

Day 66

Your Prayers Make a Difference

I urge, then, first of all, that petitions, prayers, intercession and thanksgiving be made for all people—for kings and all those in authority, that we may live peaceful and quiet lives in all godliness and holiness.

1 Timothy 2:1-2, NIV

When we pray, Paul tells us that we should pray for others. If you are like me, others are those close to us, but that isn't what the Holy Spirit had in mind when He wrote these verses through Paul. He was asking us to pray for others both inside *and* outside our journeys. Pray for "all people"—those at work, at home, at school, in government; those who lead and those who follow.

How is that possible? We can't pray for every person every day, and I don't know anyone who does or could, so what does this mean? It means that we should be open to the Spirit each time we go to pray, and we should invite Him to lead us. We may have a prayer journal or a prayer list; we should ask Him where to start and where to end. We should ask Him to lead us to cover those who need covering that day or in that season.

None of us knows what is going on in the worlds of others, particularly those of our leaders. We listen to the news, read the blogs, and we are persuaded that so and so is good or right and the other person is not. This is a huge blunder and a foolish way to live. God asks us to pray for our leaders whether we like them or not, whether we agree with them or not. I don't think any of us could imagine the pressure that the president or key senators or members of congress live under. If our leaders care about people at all, they feel pressure, and if they don't care about people, they need prayer to open their hearts to feel the pain of those they lead.

The verses say to "pray for all people—for kings [leaders] and all those in authority," and then it closes with a promise that we don't want to miss: "that we may live peaceful and quiet lives." Who doesn't want peace in the land? Many people pray for me and the other leaders at Water of Life, and I am certain that without them I wouldn't have survived the journey all these years. The possibilities of prayer run hand in hand with the promises of God, and He promises to bring peace to the land when we pray for our leaders. Our prayers make a huge difference for those we intercede for.

We are all called to pray for others, those we know and those we don't know. Don't be overwhelmed by this. Go to the Lord and ask Him to guide you, and He will direct you regarding how and who to pray for each day.

PRAYER

Holy Spirit, help me not to be overwhelmed by the thought of praying for "all people," but teach me to be led in prayer each day by You. Where You lead me, I will pray. Thank You, Father, for giving me Your promises to remind me that my prayers matter. Amen.

Day 67

Interceding for Others

I asked them about the Jews who had returned there from captivity and about how things were going in Jerusalem. They said to me, "Things are not going well for those who returned to the province of Judah. They are in great trouble and disgrace. The wall of Jerusalem has been torn down, and the gates have been destroyed by fire." When I heard this, I sat down and wept. In fact, for days I mourned, fasted, and prayed to the God of heaven.

Nehemiah 1:2–4, NLT

Nehemiah's response to bad news gives us a huge window into the soul of a great man. When Nehemiah heard that his people were in "great trouble" and the walls of Jerusalem torn down, he immediately responded with brokenness. The picture of him sitting down and weeping reveals a man who had deep inner strength. He was human, like we are, which means that he might have been tempted to let this bad report go and just go on with his life. After all, he had a good job in the king's court. Yet he embraced his pain and the plight of his people completely.

Nehemiah felt the pain and the sorrow of the Jews in Jerusalem. It is an amazing thing to let God break our hearts over the things that break His. This is how the world is changed. When the Holy Spirit allows us to hear news of brothers and sisters around the world who are in desperate need, how do we respond?

Nehemiah's first response was deep brokenness and sorrow, but he didn't stay there. He then ran to God, and he could only do that because he trusted God in spite of the painful news he had heard. Nehemiah was a world changer and a great man and leader not because he rose above pain but because he embraced it. Nehemiah 1:4 tells us that he mourned and fasted and prayed to the God of heaven for days.

Nehemiah's heart was for others, just as Jesus' heart is. He completely felt called to embrace these people and their pain, and he used their pain to fuel his prayers. He cried out to God, believing that his Father's heart was broken over this. He knew that when God's heart is broken for people, He sends His Spirit throughout the land, looking for people to move into the gap and pray.

Nehemiah's fasting and prayer led to breakthrough for his people. It brought forth strategies from heaven that then allowed Nehemiah to engage in the battle and bring forth life to people who were dying. This is our journey as well. God will sometimes bring news that breaks our hearts in order to get us on our knees interceding for people we don't know and have never met. When this happens to you, don't run from the pain; embrace it, and you will embrace the destiny of others in a way you may never have experienced before.

PRAYER

Holy Spirit, when You bring me news of others' pain and struggles, pour out Your grace on me so that instead of running from their pain, I will run into it. I want to be a vessel that honors You and brings life to others. Teach me as You taught Nehemiah. I want to be transformed deep inside. Amen.

Day 68

Surrendered to God

O Lord, God of heaven, the great and awesome God who keeps his covenant of unfailing love with those who love him and obey his commands, listen to my prayer! Look down and see me praying night and day for your people Israel. I confess that we have sinned against you. Yes, even my own family and I have sinned! We have sinned terribly by not obeying the commands, decrees, and regulations that you gave us through your servant Moses. Please remember what you told your servant Moses. . . . O Lord, please hear my prayer! Listen to the prayers of those of us who delight in honoring you.

Nehemiah 1:5–11, NLT

Crisis often moves us to pray. We hear news of situations that we are powerless to change, and our only recourse is prayer. On the surface this can seem like a desperate place to be, but it is actually a great position to find ourselves in. It thrusts us right into the lap of God—and our Father is always blessed when His people sit in His lap. Listen to Nehemiah as he crawled up there:

> O Lord, God of heaven, the great and awesome God who keeps his covenant of unfailing love with those who love him and obey his commands, listen to my prayer! Look down and see me praying night and day for your people Israel. (Neh. 1:5–6)

This man knew his God. He came before God with confidence in his time of need—no fear here. He came with honor and praise, not blame. He understood how God made things to work. He called God "great and awesome." That revelation didn't come to him overnight but through many trials and tears. Nehemiah knew that God keeps His promises, and he leaned into that trust.

Nehemiah was intimate with God and readily owned his weaknesses and those of his people. As far as we know, he hadn't done anything wrong. Yet he confessed, "Even my family and I have sinned!" Humility is such an important quality. Nehemiah never feared being real with God and owning his stuff. This led to intimacy with God and God entrusting a huge assignment to Nehemiah.

Nehemiah was sold out to God long before he got this bad news, since he declared, "Listen to the prayers of those of us who delight in honoring you." Apparently he had come to a position that we need to embrace: surrendering to God and honoring Him in our journeys. This sets us up for greatness in the kingdom. Jesus said, "If you love Me, you will obey Me" (see John 14:15). Yielding to God daily and surrendering our wills to Him honors Him, and it positions us to be used in great times of need, as Nehemiah was used in this dark hour of Israel's journey.

PRAYER

Holy Spirit, please teach me never to fear surrendering to the Father. I want to grow deeper with You, and I know that cannot happen as long as I am too proud to be honest with You about my struggles and needs. Pour out Your presence in my heart, and soften my hard places so that I will hunger to run to You. Amen.

Day 69

Waiting on God

My soul, wait in silence for God only, for my hope is from Him.

Psalm 62:5

Much of prayer has to do with waiting. Oh boy, we hate to wait, don't we? We are not a waiting generation. We are the "now" generation. The only problem with that is that God often asks us to wait, and this flies in the face of all we are told in our world today. Later is not better; now is better. Faster is better; slower is not. Waiting in the economy of God is crucial for growth, but in our world's mind it is a total waste of time. When we come and lay our hearts before God, He hears us, but He certainly doesn't always act right away.

David, who wrote Psalm 62, was familiar with waiting. He had been anointed king over Israel while Israel still had King Saul. He spent a number of years waiting, some of those years in caves. Later in his life he fled from his son Absalom, who was attempting to take his throne. It was likely during this time that he wrote this psalm. Once again he was waiting for God to move. We have all been there, in desperate need and crying out to God when He asks us to be still and wait. It is very difficult to hold still, but after a lifetime of waiting, David wrote in verses 1–2 of this psalm, "My soul waits in silence for God only; from Him is my salvation. He only is my rock and my salvation, my stronghold; I shall not be greatly shaken."

These short verses give us such an important lesson. We must wait because there is really nothing else we can do. We must wait because God is our only hope. We must wait because God saved us, and we can be sure that He didn't do that just to abandon us. Waiting declares to God, "You are my rock and my salvation, my stronghold," so there is no reason for us to go anywhere.

Be still and wait, but pray and keep praying, ask and keep asking. God hasn't abandoned you. He cannot; He promised He wouldn't. Don't run out and try to fix what you broke on your own power. Trust Him. Wait.

Micah 7:7 says, "I will look to the LORD; I will wait for the God of my salvation: my God will hear me" (ESV). He has heard you; now wait, and don't see waiting as a waste. It isn't. It is, in fact, empowering to wait—especially when God shows up! "Those who wait for the LORD will gain new strength; they will mount up with wings like eagles, they will run and not get tired, they will walk and not become weary" (Isa. 40:31).

PRAYER

Father, it is so easy to believe that waiting is a waste of time. I need help to rethink this. Teach me, Holy Spirit, how to wait not passively but actively. Teach me to wait and pray, believing that You will come at the right time to rescue me. Amen.

Day 70

Be Still Before God

Rest in the LORD and wait patiently for Him.

PSALM 37:7

The Hebrew word for "rest," or "be still," *damam*, is revealing when we unpack it. When we stop and wait before the Lord, He is able to do a deep and abiding work in us. This work requires waiting and often waiting some more. The Holy Spirit needs us to be still in order for Him to impart the deep things of the Father within us.

While *damam* means "be silent" or "be still," it is also translated "be astonished" or "be confounded." Only when we understand this does the word *damam* take up its full meaning: when the Spirit moves deeply in us, we are confounded and astonished at the amazing presence of the living God in us! We realize that God is not just around us, but He is also in us, His presence dwelling deep within our hearts and souls. When this happens, we are never the same.

During our times of resting in the Lord, patience does its work in us. Waiting patiently for God separates us from this life and moves eternity into our hearts. We no longer view waiting as wasted time. We receive strength to live and hungry hearts that want to worship. We have God's promise that waiting on Him will be worth it, that it is never wasted time:

> Though youths grow weary and tired, and vigorous young men stumble badly, yet those who wait for the LORD will

> gain new strength; they will mount up with wings like eagles, they will run and not get tired, they will walk and not become weary. (Isa. 40:30–31)

But it takes time alone with God to figure this out—time when we are quiet and still, allowing Him to speak. David, who wrote this psalm, understood this. He learned quietness before the Lord long before he became king, when he was still a shepherd boy guarding his father's sheep. Out of his stillness before God came a deep relationship with God and the ability to hold steady in the great tests that awaited him both before and after he became king. It also led him to repentance in those times when he failed the Lord.

If we don't take this time, we will grow weary and tired with the work set before us. We will slowly but surely grow distant from God's presence, and we will begin to fret about those around us. We will find our tempers flaring and our attitudes unsettled. We will get excited and upset over things that we used to simply walk away from.

Taking time to be still in His presence allows the Holy Spirit to deal with the places that separate our hearts from His. The lies we have harbored, the dishonesty we have allowed, the lack of transparency that has taken hold and darkened our hearts are revealed. All our secrets are exposed—and then God's healing flows. We are renewed, and our hearts and souls take wings; they begin again to rejoice in the healing and delivering hand of God.

PRAYER

Father, it is Your desire for me to wait. Teach me how vital it is to make time to honor You and wait on You. Remind me, Holy Spirit, that without waiting there is little room for Your working. Amen.

Day 71

The Spirit of Prayer

I will pour out on the house of David . . .
the Spirit of grace and of supplication.

Zechariah 12:10

Sometimes we wonder why prayer can be so tough. Why is it so hard to concentrate when we pray? Why is it so difficult to pray thoughtfully? And more than anything, why don't we pray with power? The answer to these questions is found in the person of the Holy Spirit. Many of us are afraid of Him, so we live and pray powerlessly. But He is the Spirit of Jesus. We need not fear Him. We need Him to live with power and pray with power.

The Holy Spirit's place in prayer cannot be overstated. He is called the Spirit of grace and supplication. The root of the Hebrew word for "grace" in Zechariah 12:10 is "to grant a favor." The Holy Spirit has many roles in a believer's life, but few are more important than His empowering place in prayer, His releasing of favor.

The New Testament talks over and over about the Holy Spirit and prayer. He is mentioned in multiple contexts regarding prayer:

> The Spirit also helps our weakness; for we do not know how to pray as we should, but the Spirit Himself intercedes for us with groanings too deep for words; and He who searches the hearts knows what the mind of the Spirit is, because He intercedes for the saints according to the will of God. (Rom. 8:26–27)

With all prayer and petition pray at all times in the Spirit. (Eph. 6:18)

Praying in the Holy Spirit . . . (Jude 1:20)

As hard as prayer is, we need all the help we can get. Romans tells us that the Holy Spirit prays for us. Ephesians tells us to pray in the Spirit—in His power, not our own. Jude says the same thing: don't go it alone, or you will never enjoy praying, and you will never find your prayers powerful.

I don't think it is overstating the crucial place the Holy Spirit has in prayer to say that we can gauge how deeply we are walking with the Holy Spirit by how deep our prayer lives are. The Holy Spirit is the One who leads us to the Father's presence. He is the One who shapes our hearts and our prayers. We need Him every day to empower us when we pray.

Today ask the Holy Spirit to engage with you as you pray; then listen for His voice, and follow His lead. As you read His Word, ask Him to point out promises that are there for you, and then pray those back to the Father with the confidence that only the Holy Spirit can give you.

PRAYER

Holy Spirit, please come to me and energize my prayer time with Your presence. I need You to touch me and empower me, to lead me as I pray and read Your Word. Thank You for caring so deeply for me. Amen.

DAY 72

Humility and Intimacy

Daniel answered before the king and said, "As for the mystery about which the king has inquired, neither wise men, conjurers, magicians nor diviners are able to declare it to the king. However, there is a God in heaven who reveals mysteries."

DANIEL 2:27–28

"There is a God in heaven who reveals mysteries." This astounding statement by Daniel gives us a glimpse into his relationship with the living God. What a crazy and amazing proposition that the God of the universe would share His thoughts with Daniel—and with us! Why don't we all know Him on these terms?

Daniel heard from God because he didn't take credit for the knowledge he received supernaturally. It would have been a huge temptation for him to do so, with King Nebuchadnezzar and all his power towering over him in that moment, but Daniel knew not to steal God's glory if he wanted to remain intimate with Him. When we take credit and steal glory from Jesus, we lose insight and intimacy with Him. Daniel understood this well, so he gave God all the glory and only then revealed the mystery God had shown him. This is a key to hearing the secrets of God.

Psalm 25:14 tells us that "the secret of the LORD is for those who fear Him, and He will make them know His covenant." Daniel understood that intimacy with God opens the door to insights that few receive in this life: "It is He who reveals the profound and hidden things" (Dan. 2:22). If we draw near to God, He will draw near to us and reveal His heart to us in ways we could otherwise never know. "Call to me and I will answer you, and will tell you great and hidden things that you have not known" (Jer. 33:3, ESV).

To have a Father who loves us and wants to share His deepest desires with us, His sons and daughters, should leave us in awe. Paul experienced this and spoke often of the mysteries, or secrets, of God. He actually explained why some people receive secrets from God and others do not: "Let a man so consider us, as servants of Christ and stewards of the mysteries of God. Moreover it is required in stewards that one be found faithful" (1 Cor. 4:1–2, NKJV). In order for God to impart wisdom and the depths of His heart to us, we must be found faithful! Wow!

Daniel was faithful, and God downloaded secrets to him. Paul was faithful, and God downloaded secrets to him. If you and I are faithful, God will download secrets to us. Do you want to know Him more today? Honor Him; seek after Him. Don't fear people, but fear and honor God. Fall in love with Him, and make Him your priority today, and He will reveal the depths of His heart and His secrets to you, as Paul wrote: "He made known to us the mystery of His will, according to His kind intention which He purposed in [Christ]" (Eph. 1:9).

PRAYER

Father, let me be found as Daniel was: faithful. Holy Spirit, move in me, and empower me to walk with integrity, putting God first and honoring Him above myself and others. I want to hear from You and know the mysteries of Your will. Amen.

Day 73

Success from God

O Lord, I beseech You, may Your ear be attentive to the prayer of Your servant and the prayer of Your servants who delight to revere Your name, and make Your servant successful today and grant him compassion before this man.

Nehemiah 1:11

God honors people who honor Him. Nehemiah knew this; he declared it back to God in Nehemiah 1:11 when he said, "Listen to the prayers of those of us who delight in honoring you" (NLT). Nehemiah had something we all need: honesty with God. If we could just be real with God about what we feel, what we need, and how we are doing and then believe in all God can do with us each day, the success we would experience would astound us.

Too often we are not honest with God. We beat around the bush and never get to the heart of the matter. We need to learn this deep lesson that Nehemiah knew: God is safe. He is kind. He wants truth in our innermost being. And He wants to make us successful. When we are real with God, we will have the confidence Nehemiah had to ask his heart's desire from his Father: "Please grant me success today by making the king favorable to me" (Neh. 1:11, NLT).

There is no doubt that God wants to rescue us in times of need. But He wants to do more with us than that. He wants to make each one of us a success. Nehemiah knew this about God because he lived honestly before Him. Nehemiah's goal was not riches or fame or power; his goal was honoring God and helping others.

Why wouldn't he have a deep confidence to ask God for success if those were his goals? Each of us needs confidence like this. We should go before God with certainty and cry out, "God, make me a success today at work so You will be glorified. Make me a success at home so my children will love You. Make me a success in the community so others will hear about Your greatness."

What made Nehemiah unique? Why did he end up repairing the wall in Jerusalem that had lain in ruins for 141 years? How did he end up helping heal the lives of the Jews who were so desperate and hurting? The answer lies in his heart for God and others along with his willingness to sacrifice in order to touch others and honor God. Others' pain always impacted Jesus. Others' pain must impact us. But this is expensive, isn't it? It costs us time and energy, and sometimes it costs us deep pain. But it is the way of the kingdom. It is the heart of God.

That is why Nehemiah asked God to make him a success. He knew the journey would be tough, but he also knew he could freely ask God to move miraculously to open doors that he could never open himself.

PRAYER

Holy Spirit, make me a success today! I desire to be completely honest with You, to honor You, and to live for You. I want Jesus to be magnified in my life today and every day. But that can happen only by Your supernatural touch in my life. Move with power over me, and use me to touch those around me today. Amen.

Day 74

Prayerful People Impact the World

Call to me and I will answer you and tell you great and unsearchable things you do not know.

Jeremiah 33:3, NIV

Jeremiah 33:3, a tiny little verse tucked away in the book of Jeremiah, promises that God will show His secrets to those who pray. The Hebrew word translated "Call to me" has to do with going after God and grabbing hold of Him. "Cry out to Me" is a good way to put it. Most people do everything but pray, but throughout Scripture we see pictures of people who prayed not just quick little shots pointed toward heaven but who prayed first and acted second. Such people have deeply impacted the world for Jesus.

Making the transition from acting first to praying first is tough. It flies in the face of human nature and our desire to work out life on our own terms. It flies in the face of our culture, which tells us to work and keep working. Prayer for most of us *is* work. It is tough to set aside time and go to our closet, or "inner room," shutting ourselves away from others and really calling out to God as Jesus said: "When you pray, go into your inner room, close your door and pray to your Father who is in secret, and your Father who sees what is done in secret will reward you" (Matt. 6:6). Prayer is tough, and it takes a disciplined and hungry spirit to accomplish;

but for those who decide to do it, it is worth it to see lives changed and hearts and circumstances altered.

Many years ago I heard of such a man, and I made it a point to read about his life. His name was David Livingstone. He is celebrated for many things, but for me he was famous from the cartoons I had watched as a child in which people went hunting for him in deepest, darkest Africa, approaching every white man they met and saying, "Dr. Livingstone, I presume?" David Livingstone accomplished far more in Africa than any of us could ever have imagined because of one thing: he prayed and prayed and prayed some more. Every year on his birthday he wrote a prayer, and the last year of his life, this is what he wrote: "O Divine One, I have not loved Thee earnestly, deeply, sincerely enough. Grant, I pray Thee, that before this year is ended I may have finished the task."[2]

At the end of that year, David Livingstone died. When his followers looked into his tent, they found him dead on his knees beside his bed. Yes, he literally died praying! When the British came to claim his body and bury him in Westminster Abbey, they found that those he had touched had cut his heart out and buried it in Africa. They told the British, "You may have his body, but his heart was always with us in Africa, so it will remain here."[3] David Livingstone was an amazing man who grasped the magnitude of taking hold of God to change the world.

PRAYER

Holy Spirit, teach me to hunger to pray. Let me not see it as a labor but as a blessing that can and will change my life and the lives of those around me. Amen.

Day 75

Signs and Wonders

I want you all to know about the miraculous signs and wonders the Most High God has performed for me. How great are his signs, how powerful his wonders! His kingdom will last forever, his rule through all generations.

DANIEL 4:2–3, NLT

We serve a wonderfully powerful God, One who delights in moving with signs and wonders in our midst. God's miracles, supernatural insight, and healing have always been used as signs to point us in His direction. A sign helps to steer our journeys; God uses signs to do the same in our lives.

King Nebuchadnezzar experienced an assortment of God's signs and wonders, including watching four men walk around in a fiery furnace, having his dreams read and interpreted by Daniel, and losing his kingdom and having it restored to him. Now, as an old man, he wanted the people of his kingdom to know "how great are His signs, how powerful His wonders!"

When I first met Jesus, I often lay on my bed in my bedroom and read a little paraphrased Bible called *Good News for Modern Man*. It was an easy read with no "thees" or "thous," just simple English, but that wasn't the key. The sign that led me to Jesus was His Spirit showing up every time I opened that book, breathing life into my dead room. I literally talked to His presence when I read, asking, "What are You doing here?" "Who are You?" "What do You want with me?" Over and over He brooded over me, and a depth of love and care I had never known rose up inside me. It was supernatural, and it got my attention and ultimately my surrender. Since then I have been graciously blessed to experience many signs and wonders in my journey with Jesus, as many of you have as well.

As Nebuchadnezzar's words show, he was a wise old man. He had not only experienced the miraculous signs and wonders of God, but he was now declaring them to others. This is what living in Jesus should do to all of us. It should miraculously touch us deep inside and humble us as it did Nebuchadnezzar. Then in that humility, praise and adoration should come forth as it did with the king. He wanted to tell others of the greatness of God. This is exactly why God uses signs and wonders: to display His greatness toward us and in us so we can declare it to others.

The only way we can and will remember how great God has been to us is to journal—to write down the miraculous things God has done for us in our journeys. We are all forgetful; unfortunately we often wonder, *What have You done for me today, God?* instead of remembering His powerful touch and praising Him for it. Stop today and remember the signs from God that have brought you into His presence. Write them down. Thank Him for them, and speak out His greatness to others when you have the opportunity. It will enlarge His hand and His presence every day in your journey.

PRAYER

Holy Spirit, You have done so many wild and miraculous things both in me and in those around me. Thank You! Today I praise You and honor Your touch in my life. Amen.

Day 76

Tune in to God

They brought the gold vessels that had been taken out of the temple, the house of God which was in Jerusalem; and the king and his nobles, his wives and his concubines drank from them. They drank the wine and praised the gods of gold and silver, of bronze, iron, wood and stone.

Daniel 5:3–4

A while back my family and I went on a three-day cruise. We had an enjoyable time except for the one day when the weather was rough and I became nauseated and pretty much could not do anything. You see, when the cruise took off, the captain came on the public audio system and told us that we would be changing course the next day due to rough weather ahead. My family and I didn't think much about this, because this was our first cruise ever! But seasoned cruise-ship travelers prepared for the rough seas by applying anti-nausea patches behind their ears. When the ship started going side to side the next day, they were not as impacted by it as I was! Although I hadn't ignored the warning from the captain, I was not prepared for the storm when it came.

Many times we miss signs and cues in front of us because we either look past them or simply ignore them. God puts signs in front of us every day to guide us on the right path. If we tune in to Him by spending time at His feet every day, reading the Word and meditating upon His statutes, we won't miss those signs.

King Belshazzar not only missed God's signs—he flatly ignored them. He did things that were clearly abominable in the sight of the Lord by drinking out of the gold vessels taken from the temple of the house of the Lord and praising gods of gold and silver, bronze and iron, wood and stone. We too sometimes ignore God's Word and do what brings pleasure to us rather than to God. In fact, the Bible warns us in Proverbs 29:1, "A man who hardens his neck after much reproof will suddenly be broken beyond remedy."

If we've ignored God's signs, it's not too late for us. Blessedly, God is full of grace and forgiveness. John 3:16 says that "God so loved the world, that He gave His only begotten Son, that whoever believes in Him shall not perish, but have eternal life." And 2 Timothy 2:21 reminds us, "If anyone cleanses himself from [dishonorable] things, he will be a vessel for honor, sanctified, useful to the Master, prepared for every good work." Who doesn't want eternal life and useful service for God?

The best way to stay in tune with God is to do what Daniel did: worship the living God every day and keep ourselves pure in the midst of a culture that often does not follow God. Try it today, and see how full your heart will be!

PRAYER

Lord, I pray that You will give me a heart that is sensitive to Your voice. Please take out my heart of stone, and give me a heart of flesh so that I will listen to and obey Your voice every day. Amen.

Day 77

God's Timing

I waited patiently for the L*ORD*.

Psalm 40:1

One of the first lessons God attempts to teach His people is to wait for His timing. David had to learn this lesson during his years of running from King Saul when Saul wanted to kill him. David was anointed king as a young man, but it would be years before it was time for him to take the throne. None of us likes to wait, nor are we inclined to wait patiently, although some of us will yield to it if we are forced. But many of us do not understand the critical importance of God's timing. We look with eyes of flesh and fail to see God's hand moving in the spiritual realm even as we wait. We consider our circumstances in our own minds and lose sight of the things that are unseen.

Israel battled the same weaknesses. That's why God set the pace for them:

> Sometimes the cloud stayed only overnight and lifted the next morning. But day or night, when the cloud lifted, the people broke camp and moved on. Whether the cloud stayed above the Tabernacle for two days, a month, or a year, the people of Israel stayed in camp and did not move on. But as soon as it lifted, they broke camp and moved on. (Num. 9:21–22, NLT)

This was Israel's journey. They were led by the cloud by day and the fire by night. If the cloud didn't move, neither did they. Imagine getting up each day with no plan, no itinerary, no direction all. God was trying to teach these people who had lived for four hundred years in Egypt with very little faith how to trust Him. And what was the key lesson for them? Waiting. It is the same for us today. If we want to walk with Jesus, we'd better figure on waiting. He will make us wait. And why? To teach us to trust. To teach us not to move until the cloud moves.

Many of us think, *No way! God would never do that to me. He would never just ask me to wait.* Oh yes, He would, and He does. He did it to David and other godly men and women in the Bible. The problem is, we often don't listen to Him. We walk ahead without the cloud and the fire—with no covering and no protection.

Is it tough to wait? Absolutely. But it is foolish not to. This lesson of waiting is so important to our faith and trust, because without waiting neither will grow. Waiting builds both faith and trust. It teaches us about God's timing and how crucial it is to our success.

Learning to wait is foundational to all the other lessons God wants to teach us. Without waiting there is no promised land. Without waiting there is no deliverance from jealous enemies. Without waiting miracles cease, and God's plan is lost. Faith and trust grow when we yield to the Lord's ways and timing and surrender our own.

PRAYER

Holy Spirit, teach me the value of waiting. I always want to pick the fruit before it is ripe. Forgive me for not yielding to You and Your ways more quickly. Please pour out Your grace and power on me so that I will learn the huge lesson of waiting. Amen.

Day 78

Stay Close to Jesus

Remain in me, as I also remain in you. No branch can bear fruit by itself; it must remain in the vine. Neither can you bear fruit unless you remain in me.

John 15:4, NIV

All effective prayer must be born out of relationship with our Father, empowered by His Spirit. When we pray this way, God imparts His authority to us, and our prayers become His possibility. That cannot take place without us being found in Him. Many of us wander in and out of our relationship with Jesus, and as we wander away from Him, our prayers also wander and weaken. In order to effectively pray, we must be found in relationship with Jesus.

In John 15 Jesus taught His followers how vital it would be for them to remain close to Him; in order for them to flourish, they would have to abide in Him:

> Remain in me, as I also remain in you. No branch can bear fruit by itself; it must remain in the vine. Neither can you bear fruit unless you remain in me.
>
> I am the vine; you are the branches. If you remain in me and I in you, you will bear much fruit; apart from me you can do nothing. If you do not remain in me, you are like a branch that is thrown away and withers; such branches are picked up, thrown into the fire and burned. If you remain in me and my words remain in you, ask whatever you wish,

> and it will be done for you. This is to my Father's glory, that you bear much fruit, showing yourselves to be my disciples.
>
> As the Father has loved me, so have I loved you. Now remain in my love. If you keep my commands, you will remain in my love, just as I have kept my Father's commands and remain in His love. I have told you this so that my joy may be in you and that your joy may be complete. (John 15:4–11, NIV)

When Jesus said to "remain," or abide, He used the word *meno*. It means to stay in—not to wander but to remain with Him. He used this word nine times in these verses. Clearly it is important for us to be with Jesus if we are to pray effectively. People who make a difference, who bring breakthrough, have lives that count and matter. They make intentional time for prayer, believing that God can do what we can never do.

PRAYER

Holy Spirit, I find abiding and remaining in Christ so difficult sometimes. My heart really is prone to wander. Teach me and empower me to stay in, to love Jesus with a whole heart, and to be effective and intentional in my prayer life. Amen.

Day 79

You Have Not Because You Ask Not

The king said to me, "What would you request?" So I prayed to the God of heaven. I said to the king, "If it please the king, and if your servant has found favor before you, send me to Judah, to the city of my fathers' tombs, that I may rebuild it." Then the king said to me, . . . "How long will your journey be, and when will you return?" So it pleased the king to send me, and I gave him a definite time. And I said to the king, "If it please the king, let letters be given me for the governors of the provinces beyond the River, that they may allow me to pass through until I come to Judah, and a letter to Asaph the keeper of the king's forest, that he may give me timber to make beams for the gates . . . for the wall of the city and for the house to which I will go." And the king granted them to me because the good hand of my God was on me.

Nehemiah 2:4–8

Nehemiah's request of King Artaxerxes details an incredible interaction between a cupbearer and a king. It was highly unusual as well as risky, especially since the king had earlier written a letter forbidding any more building in Jerusalem (see Ezra 4:11–23). But this was typical Nehemiah, taking a huge risk and looking out for others above himself. Over and over he did this, even when it put him in danger, as this discussion did. People who do things like this are the people Jesus described when He said, "Anyone who believes in me may come and drink! For the Scriptures declare, 'Rivers of living water will flow from his heart'" (John 7:38, NLT).

Nehemiah's life overflowed. His heart was full of love for God and for people. This is why God put him in a place where he could make a difference for others. His life, like Joseph's, Moses', Daniel's, and Paul's, tells a story: we were created for something bigger than just living. We need to believe that the "good hand of God" is on us.

Nehemiah was both prayerful and strategic in his thinking. These two traits allowed him time and again to rise above the crowd and lead with the heart of God. When the king asked him what he wanted, he did not hesitate. He had his list ready, and he laid it out before the king. His request was big, but the Bible is clear in James 4:2: "You do not have because you do not ask." Nehemiah asked, and God moved.

Do you ask? Do you believe God wants to move in your destiny? Do you believe, as Nehemiah did of his own life, that God has His hand on you? He does. He hungers to touch you and then use you to touch others. Start each day with faith that God has His hand on you and that He can do far and above all that you could ask or think (see Eph. 3:20–21). Run to Him, and believe that He will move in you.

PRAYER

Jesus, I often doubt that You really want to move with power in me. Forgive me for my unbelief. Teach me, Holy Spirit, to call upon You and to trust that You will move in me throughout this day. Amen.

Day 80

Ask God

Ask of Me, and I will surely give the nations as Your inheritance.

Psalm 2:8

The kingdom of God is built on the principle of asking. But many of us struggle with asking, seeing it as a weakness rather than a strength. Asking takes our problem out of our hands and puts it into God's. Asking kills self-reliance and teaches us to lean on Jesus.

James Gilmore, a British missionary to China, once said,

> Surely a day asking of God to overrule all events for good is not lost. Still there is a great feeling that when a person is praying they are doing nothing, and this feeling makes us give undue importance to work, sometimes even to the hurrying over or even to the neglect of prayer.[4]

We are in danger every day of not trusting God, not relying on Him. It is so easy for us to rely on ourselves, but that will never build our spirits. We grow spiritually only by depending on Him. Can't God still do for us today what He did for Elijah and Elisha? For Peter and Paul? Is His ability to help us and move our mountains less than it was in their days?

God works today the same way He did in the days of old: by prayer. Prayer moves God to work in our circumstances, but we must settle it in our hearts that asking is the condition of God moving. When we throw up weak and thoughtless prayers, all we are really saying is that we don't believe God cares and will move. But when we go to His throne with confidence, asking specifically for what we need to see Him do each day, we position ourselves for Him to move.

Asking is a condition of dependence. And our dependence on God moves His heart to enter into our circumstances, however difficult they may be. James 5:17–18 tells us, "Elijah was as human as we are, and yet when he prayed earnestly that no rain would fall, none fell for three and a half years! Then, when he prayed again, the sky sent down rain and the earth began to yield its crops" (NLT). Elijah was a prophet and a powerful one at that. Yet the Bible makes it clear that he was human like us, and when he asked, his Father changed his world.

If you doubt that you could actually make a difference today, ask the Holy Spirit to reveal His desires to you. The Holy Spirit has the power you and I lack when we come to prayer—the power to believe beyond ourselves, to engage Satan when he confronts us or our families. The Holy Spirit is the spirit of prayer that we all need when asking seems beyond us.

PRAYER

Father, teach me to ask and never be ashamed to ask. Help me to come to You with confidence that You care, that You listen, and that You, Holy Spirit, want to empower me to pray and ask with a boldness I have never known. Touch me today, I ask, and empower me to pray. Amen.

DAY 81

Ask to Touch Others

Ask for whatever you want me to give you.

2 CHRONICLES 1:7, NIV

Shortly after Solomon became king over Israel, God told him, "Ask for whatever you want me to give you." Solomon was fully committed to his God at this time. What did the new king ask for?

What would you have asked for? When you pray, what sort of things *do* you ask God for? Second Chronicles 1:10 tells us what Solomon requested: "Give me wisdom and knowledge, that I may lead this people, for who is able to govern this great people of yours?" (NIV). This young king asked for wisdom and knowledge to help others! Amazingly, he didn't ask for riches or gold or power or fame or anything to enhance his own life. God was so taken by Solomon's heart for others that He granted him not only the wisdom and knowledge he asked for but also riches and gold. God desires truth in our innermost beings, and He is looking for hearts that desire to serve others and glorify Him.

When we pray, we should not limit God to our small situations, because He asks us to touch others and change the world. When He finds a heart that is more concerned for others than for self, He pours out His blessings.

Andrew Murray, who wrote many books on prayer, said this:

> In your prayers, above everything else, beware of limiting God, not only through unbelief but also by thinking you

> know exactly what He can do. Learn to expect the unexpected, beyond all you ask or think. So each time you intercede through prayer, first be quiet and worship God in His glory. Think of what He can do, how He delights in Christ His Son, and of your place in Him, then expect great things.[5]

Solomon asked for a great thing—wisdom and knowledge to help God's people—and God more than answered him. Why would He do less for us? Prayer can heal others as well as us. It can build life in the broken hearts of those we have never met as quickly as it can heal our own wounds. Prayer can move an army of angels or a hard human heart if we will come in faith for our Father's will to be done and His kingdom to come on Earth as it is in heaven.

Give yourself to prayer, and you give yourself to God. Give yourself to God, and you will see captives set free and bondage broken, hearts healed, and lives restored. Satan cannot stand against the fervent prayers of a righteous person. Make your life a prayer like Elijah's when he knelt on Mount Carmel and put his face to the ground and cried out to God (see 1 Kings 18:41-45). You will not be disappointed!

PRAYER

Father, make my life a life of prayer. Teach me, Holy Spirit, to believe for great things for others, to pray for others, and to believe for others. I hunger to see You move today with the same power You have moved throughout history to change destinities. Amen.

Day 82

Authority in Prayer

This, then, is how you should pray: . . . "Your kingdom come, Your will be done, on earth as it is in heaven."

Matthew 6:9–10, NIV

When Jesus was asked by His followers to teach them to pray, He began with "Our Father," but then He quickly moved on to "Your kingdom come, Your will be done on earth as it is in heaven." Wow, what a leap—from intimate relationship to massive authority.

For God's will to be done on Earth, there must be a huge battle, because Earth is the realm of Satan. He was cast down from heaven to Earth, and he has real and deep authority here. In Luke 4:6–7 Satan talks about his spiritual authority when speaking to Jesus of the kingdoms of the earth: "I will give you all their authority and splendor; it has been given to me, and I can give it to anyone I want to. If you worship me, it will all be yours" (NIV).

When Jesus said to pray for God's kingdom to come and His will to be done on Earth as it is in heaven, He was contrasting heaven's wonderful possibilities with what we know takes place on Earth. He was also saying that praying makes Earth a lot more like heaven. So we should pray for God's kingdom to come here to our homes and lives. His kingdom has to do with His rule. Kings rule, and kingdoms are the areas they rule over. Jesus is asking us to pray for His authority to replace Satan's authority in our journeys today in real and tangible ways.

Our prayers can make a huge difference in marriages, in children's lives, in broken hearts, and in war-ravaged countries. So pray, and pray believing that God will come and that His will would be done to heal and restore, renew and rebuild what hell has torn down. Our decisions to pray can do this. Our prayers impact eternity for countless other people—those we know and can see and those we may never meet.

Jesus said in Luke 10:19, "I have given you authority . . . to overcome all the power of the enemy" (NIV). There is no question about whether or not we can win this war; the question is, will we pray? And will we pray specifically and intentionally for God's will to be done in circumstances and situations that desperately need His touch?

This type of prayer is only effective if the Holy Spirit leads the way, so stop and pray, and wait and listen for His voice. Open the Word of God, and believe that the Lord will show up today in your prayer life as He did in the early church. "While they were ministering to the Lord and fasting, the Holy Spirit said, 'Set apart for Me Barnabas and Saul for the work to which I have called them'" (Acts 13:2–4).

PRAYER

Father, move in me today as You moved in the early church. Holy Spirit, I believe that You have given me authority to bring the kingdom of God to circumstances that I could never change. Move in me and through me as I pray. Amen.

Day 83

Boldness in Prayer

Bend down, O Lord, and hear my prayer; answer me,
for I need your help. Protect me, for I am devoted to you.
Save me, for I serve you and trust you. You are my God.
Be merciful to me, O Lord, for I am calling on you constantly.
Give me happiness, O Lord, for I give myself to you. O Lord,
you are so good, so ready to forgive, so full of unfailing love for
all who ask for your help. Listen closely to my prayer, O Lord;
hear my urgent cry. I will call to you whenever I'm in trouble,
and you will answer me.

Psalm 86:1–7, NLT

I have heard many teachings on prayer, but none of them taught me to tell God how devoted I am to Him, how much I trust Him, how much I love Him. It appears almost awkward to declare such things to God. If I were honest, I'd have to say that I dwell far too much on the times when I am not devoted or trusting than on the times I am. David, on the other hand, arrived at a starkly candid place with God during his journey with Him. He was completely forthright with God in his prayer life. In order for us to mature in prayer, honesty and boldness are essential.

David had been stripped bare of the prideful attitudes that affect so many of us. His pain had been long and deep, and it taught him boldness with God: "Bend down and listen to me; answer me. I need Your help." This sounds almost childlike. I mean, isn't this how a child talks to his or her mom? David then told God of his devotion, his service, and his trust. It was as if he was saying, "I have given myself to You, and there is nowhere else for me to go, so help me."

But the core of all that drove David in prayer is that he knew the heart and character of God. Over and over we see this in him: "O Lord, You are so good, so ready to forgive, so full of unfailing love for all who ask for Your help." We are apt to think that this was just David being David, but he was clearly choosing to honor God while under huge duress (see Ps. 86:14–15).

This is the key to prayer that really takes hold of God: knowing that our prayer is tied to His character, not our circumstances. Keeping our eyes on our Father under pressure is hard for many of us. We allow our pain and the presence of our enemies to overwhelm us, just as hell hopes we will. Instead we should cry out to God as David did: "Bend down and listen to me; answer me. I need Your help." When we set our eyes on Jesus in this way, we are making a declaration: "You will answer me." What confidence, what hope under pressure! This is the pathway for each of us. Don't give into despair; give into God's greatness!

PRAYER

Father, I believe that by the power of Your Spirit You can put the same faith in me that David brought to You in prayer. I want to grab hold of Your character and goodness and never let go! Amen.

Day 84

God's Power Within Us

To Him who is able to do far more abundantly beyond all that we ask or think, according to the power that works within us, to Him be the glory in the church and in Christ Jesus to all generations forever and ever. Amen.

Ephesians 3:20-21

What can God do for us? If we come to Him with our prayers and lay out our lives before Him, what can He do for us? He can do for us exactly as much as we allow Him to.

Some people spend their whole lives running to God only in times of crisis or need. They have no intention of letting Him direct their steps or influence their journeys. They desire Him only to save them from the messes they get themselves into. Yet God tells us clearly that He isn't our cleanup man. He isn't an errand boy we can direct at our whim. He is our God. He is the author and finisher of our faith. He is jealous for us. His love for us is deep—deeper than we will ever know this side of heaven.

When we yield to His love, God answers prayers in ways we can never imagine possible. He is certainly able to do "far more abundantly," or as one translation puts it, "exceedingly abundantly beyond all we ask or think." Paul chose an incredible word to say this: *huperekperissou*. It is three Greek terms woven together to give it a huge impact and to say that God can work "far more abundantly"—beyond our wildest dreams—if only we will allow Him to have His way in us. That is the condition put on this promise.

Answered prayer only happens "according to the power that works within us." If there is little or no power working within us, we will see little or no response to our cries. God is not limited; we are. His resources are infinite, amazing, and limitless. But He has chosen to make us partners in eternity and in prayer, and we control how much He can do with our prayers by how much we allow Him to do in our lives. The choice is simple: we need to invite God in every day, all the time. We need to open up the closets of our hearts and ask the Holy Spirit to move in every part of us. As we surrender to Him daily, through our prayers we will watch His power move at levels we have only dreamed of in our lives.

This is actually a pretty good deal, because we will get blessed in two different ways: First, our lives will be touched more deeply than ever before as the peace of God takes up residency in us. Second, our prayers will be answered "far more abundantly" than we could even ask or think. Why not begin today? Yield that area you are holding onto, that relationship you know is not healthy, that desire that always seems to get you into trouble, and let God start fresh and new in you today.

PRAYER

Father, why am I so fearful of allowing You into every area of my life? Holy Spirit, today I declare, "I yield my life to You." Please, Father, have Your way in me. Amen.

Day 85

Importunity

Ask and it will be given to you; seek and you will find; knock and the door will be opened to you.

Matthew 7:7, NIV

Asking can be such a natural thing. We grow up asking our parents for food, help, the car, money. But when it comes to God and asking, we often miss the mark. We might ask Him for what we want or need, but when Jesus said, "Ask and it will be given to you; seek and you will find; knock and the door will be opened to you," He was defining a different kind of asking.

Asking in the Bible has to do with taking hold of God and clinging to Him, believing that He and He alone has what we need. Jesus taught this lesson in the first message He preached (see Matt. 7:7–11). He was trying to help people reorient their thinking about God—who He was and what life in Him was really about. He included three steps to taking hold of God: ask, seek, and knock. These have to do with wrestling with God over issues and life, knowing that if He alone has what we need, we will stay in and keep asking, keep seeking, and keep knocking. There is an old-school word for this kind of asking: "importunity." It means to hold on, to press on, to wait with a relentless grasp of something. In this case, that something is God.

In Mark 7:25–30 a lady whose daughter was demonized came to Jesus for help. First He denied her His presence. Then He denied her request. But she wouldn't give up. She was relentless, and she won the day with her importunity. Her insistence grabbed Jesus' heart, and He yielded to her request. Because she was so filled with faith, she would not take no for an answer. What an amazing thought.

Perseverance with God is found all over Scripture. Elijah in 1 Kings 18:42–43 exercised the same kind of tenacity:

> Elijah went up to the top of Carmel; and he crouched down on the earth and put his face between his knees. He said to his servant, "Go up now, look toward the sea." So he went up and looked and said, "There is nothing." And he said, "Go back" seven times.

Seven times Elijah prayed and sent his servant to check on the clouds, and six times there was nothing. I certainly would have given up, but Elijah didn't, and he prevailed! Not because he was so godly or great but because he was persistent. He asked and asked and kept asking, because asking is the law of the kingdom.

Come to your Father with boldness. Take hold of His heart, and ask. Moses did this for the people of Israel when he fasted for forty days and prayed. Jesus did this for us when He went to the garden and prayed. You and I can and should do this too. Don't give up! Press on, and press in. Your Father waits for you.

PRAYER

Father, teach me to stay in and not give up. Help me believe that You love me and want me to come and keep coming, even when I don't get an answer immediately. Thank You that You love for me to come and chase after You. Amen.

Day 86

Remind God of His Promises

Remember, Lord, how I have walked before you faithfully and with wholehearted devotion and have done what is good in your eyes.

2 Kings 20:3, NIV

Sometimes we forget what really matters. An important principle found all over the Bible is remembering. Remembering is what Jesus had in mind His last night on Earth when He first took the Passover cup and instituted communion as we know it today. He said, "Do this in remembrance of Me" (Luke 22:19).

The Bible is full of promises that God has made to us, His people, and He expects us to pray them out in our circumstances. These promises remind us that God has spoken and that He keeps His word. When we pray, we should remind God of His promises. Hezekiah reminded God of His promises in prayer when he was terminally ill and ran to God for help:

> About that time Hezekiah became deathly ill, and the prophet Isaiah son of Amoz went to visit him. He gave the king this message: "This is what the Lord says: Set your affairs in order, for you are going to die. You will not recover from this illness."
>
> When Hezekiah heard this, he turned his face to the wall and prayed to the Lord, "Remember, O Lord, how I

> have always been faithful to you and have served you single-mindedly, always doing what pleases you." Then he broke down and wept bitterly.
>
> But before Isaiah had left the middle courtyard, this message came to him from the LORD: "Go back to Hezekiah, the leader of my people. Tell him, 'This is what the LORD, the God of your ancestor David, says: I have heard your prayer and seen your tears. I will heal you, and three days from now you will get out of bed and go to the temple of the LORD.'" (2 Kings 20:1–5, NLT)

Hezekiah is a great example of a praying person who reminded God of His situation. The words "Remember, O Lord" are more powerful than most of us would believe, because they are packed full of faith. "Remember, God, what You said"; "Remember, God, what I did"; "Remember, God!" God never forgets, so this isn't really about Him remembering; it is about us engaging in His promises and His character as Hezekiah did. It is declaring, "I trust You! Do something."

In order to engage in God's promises, we have to engage in His Word. It is there that we find His promises. It is there that we will find the answer for our need that we can take to Him in prayer and remind Him that we know that His promises are for us today!

PRAYER

Holy Spirit, taking hold of a promise the Father has made and then reminding Him of it are not things I always do. Help me have the confidence and faith to grab hold of the Word and the promises I need today and then to pray them back to You. Amen.

DAY 87

Don't Quit!

He was telling them a parable to show that at all times they ought to pray and not to lose heart.

LUKE 18:1

Our hearts are funny and fickle. They chase after so many worthless things, and when they do decide to do good, to be generous and loving, we often grow weary of doing good. Thankfully, when we turn away from the Lord, the same thing often happens with our hearts: they grow weary of doing bad, and we come home. But the truth is, our hearts run from one thing to the next looking for comfort, security, fun, excitement, and pleasure.

For people to be touched by God, we must pray. We see that principle in full force at Pentecost. Jesus sent His followers to prayer, and they prayed and waited and prayed and waited—for days. Acts 1:14 tells us, "They all joined together constantly in prayer, along with the women and Mary the mother of Jesus, and with his brothers" (NIV). This went on for likely upwards of ten days!

It is easy to lose heart when we pray, to just give up and surrender to our reality and say, "He's not coming, or He would already have arrived." But Jesus told us in Luke 18 about a widow who comes to a judge and asks for protection. The judge doesn't care about the woman, so he does nothing for her—yet her persistence begins to take a toll on him. Finally he says to himself, "Because this widow bothers me, I will give her legal protection, otherwise by continually coming she will wear me out" (Luke 18:5). Then Jesus essentially said this: "Don't give up; don't lose heart when you pray. Stay in, even when everything and everybody says to give up."

How long should we pray for something? The answer is quite simple: pray and keep believing until what we ask for happens or until God gives us the assurance that He has heard our cries and we can stop. That is the only way we will know it is time to stop. Otherwise, we should keep praying.

Scripture is clear that hell hates for us to pray, and Satan works overtime to thwart our prayers. So don't give up! Press in, and believe beyond what you can see. Intercession is a powerful weapon against hell and the work of the enemy, so keep praying, and don't lose heart.

PRAYER

Father, teach me to persist in prayer and not lose heart. Holy Spirit, empower me and raise my faith level so that even when I cannot see answers to my prayers, I don't lose faith. Amen.

Day 88

Prayer Effects Real Change

I gave my attention to the LORD God to seek Him by prayer and supplications, with fasting, sackcloth and ashes. . . . In those days, I, Daniel, had been mourning for three entire weeks. I did not eat any tasty food, nor did meat or wine enter my mouth, nor did I use any ointment at all until the entire three weeks were completed. . . . "Do not be afraid, Daniel, for from the first day that you set your heart on understanding this and on humbling yourself before your God, your words were heard, and I have come in response to your words."

DANIEL 9:3; 10:2–12

These stories in Daniel 9–10 are rather astounding ones packed full of principles on prayer. First, Daniel was compelled to cry out to God on behalf of his people (see Dan. 9:3–19). Clearly, we know that we need to pray not only for ourselves but for the injustice others face. Second, Daniel prayed and fasted for three weeks without an answer. But he didn't give up! He pressed in and believed beyond what he could see or touch, and finally the answer came and clarified his whole ordeal: Satan had thwarted God's response. There is a battle in the spiritual realm, and if you are a believer in Jesus, a Christ follower, then you are part of that battle.

You can be sure that hell will do everything it can to stop your prayers and discourage your prayer life.

Beyond these two principles, Daniel understood something vital to effective prayer: his prayers made a difference. There are two types of Christians. First are the Christians who pray and ask God to simply help them get through their circumstances, whatever they are: "Help me do my best, and give me help and peace when I go through this." The second type believes their prayers can alter their circumstances and the circumstances of others. One believes life is a chance; the other believes it is under a sovereign design. The whole of the book of Daniel declares that God is in control, sovereign, yet Daniel participated in God's sovereignty through his prayers.

I know a dear lady who prays like this. During 2017 Joy Dawson daily interceded for my life, as she had for some time. On July 6 at 3:25 p.m., my phone rang. It was Joy, and she said, "The Lord gave me a passage for you, but telling you is a risk, because the passage declares healing over you, and you're not sick." Well, I *was* sick, and I had never told Joy, but Jesus had! Here is part of the passage: "I will heal him; I will lead him and restore comfort to him and to his mourners, creating the praise of the lips" (Isa. 57:18–19).

God is calling some of you to come to terms with your power and potential in prayer. Yield to Him, and touch others as Daniel and Joy did. You will be blessed beyond your wildest dreams.

PRAYER

Father, Your power and possibilities are not reserved for an elite group of people but for those people who believe You. Teach me, Holy Spirit, to be one of those people who believe that prayer can and does change the world. Amen.

DAY 89

Battling Through

A hand touched me and lifted me, still trembling, to my hands and knees. . . . Then he said, "Don't be afraid, Daniel. Since the first day you began to pray for understanding and to humble yourself before your God, your request has been heard in heaven. I have come in answer to your prayer. But for twenty-one days the spirit prince of the kingdom of Persia blocked my way. Then Michael, one of the archangels, came to help me, and I left him there with the spirit prince of the kingdom of Persia."

DANIEL 10:10-13, NLT

Daniel had been fasting and praying for his people for twenty-one days. As far as we know, he had done nothing that should have hindered his prayer life, but still his prayers went unanswered. This has happened to all of us. What we often overlook when we are praying for others is that Satan hates them and is doing all he can to thwart our prayers for them.

This is one of the clearest examples in the Bible of what spiritual warfare actually looks like. As far as we can see, Daniel's prayer was answered as soon as he prayed, but Daniel didn't get the response for three weeks because the Prince of Persia, or the spirit that reigned over Persia, blocked the angel's way. God had immediately sent an angelic response to Daniel's prayer, but a battle ensued in the heavenly realm that kept the answer from coming. This left Daniel alone and empty on Earth, wondering what had happened and where God was in his struggle.

We have all been there, haven't we? We have prayed and believed, and all was quiet. Most of us have thought, *If God loves me and cares for me, why hasn't He answered me?* At times like this it is so important to remember what Ephesians 6:12 tells us: "Our struggle is not against flesh and blood, but against the rulers, against the powers, against the world forces of this darkness, against the spiritual forces of wickedness in the heavenly places."

In Daniel 9:3 we see Daniel giving himself to prayer for his people. This is something we all do for those we love. But when we pray for others, or intercede, as the Bible calls it, we place ourselves in the midst of whatever battle they are facing. This is exactly what Daniel did. He loved his people and prayed for them, and his prayers for them brought him face to face with a stark reality: Satan hates people and will do whatever he can to hinder and destroy them. Daniel, on the other hand, loved God and people, so he gave himself to intercession and prayer.

God's call for us is to love and pray for others, but it is vital to remember that when we pray, we are entering into the battle for others' lives and destinies. Do not be easily discouraged. Take heart and press in, knowing that the battle rages on and that your prayers are a crucial part of fulfilling others' destinies!

PRAYER

Father, when I pray, remind me that I am entering a spiritual battlefield. Remind me that a war rages on in the spiritual realm for lives and destinies and that my prayers make a huge difference for others. Amen.

DAY 90

Dare to Prove the Greatness of God

Peter was kept in prison, but the church was earnestly praying to God for him.

ACTS 12:5, NIV

What a picture. Peter, the one whom Jesus had chosen to help lead a small band of believers to change the world, was in a huge crisis. Arrested and imprisoned by King Herod, no doubt he would soon be killed:

> King Herod arrested some who belonged to the church, intending to persecute them. He had James, the brother of John, put to death with the sword. When he saw that this met with approval among the Jews, he proceeded to seize Peter also. (Acts 12:1–3, NIV)

Peter was as good as dead in the hands of Herod. Herod had already killed James and had seen a favorable response to his death. Peter wasn't long for this world, but "the church was earnestly praying for him." What a statement, "the church." We hear so many negative things about the church today, how bad organized religion is and such, but here the church was being what God intended it to be. Jesus said in Matthew 21:13, "It is written, 'My house shall be called a house of prayer.'" We His people, the church, are called to pray.

We are equipped by God's Spirit to pray, and we have great and powerful promises that when we pray, God will move. Prayer is our link to God's heart and His power. It makes a way over every obstacle that stands against His work. We see this as Peter's story unfolds: Peter was sleeping in prison when an angel awakened him and told him to get up and walk out of there. His chains fell off, and the prison doors opened. In Acts 12:23, wicked King Herod was in fact the one who died, not Peter, all because the church prayed.

Do we have any idea of the power God has put in our midst through prayer? A. B. Simpson said, "He is looking not for great people but for people who will dare to prove the greatness of their God!"[6] We are called to make a difference in our world, and it cannot be done without prayer—earnest prayer. The word "earnestly" in Acts 12:5 is an important one. The church was praying "earnestly," or fervently. "Earnestly" comes from one of my favorite words in the New Testament, *ektenos*. It means to stretch out. The church was fervently praying, and it was stretching people out.

This is what we are called to do. We are to stretch out for others in crisis, for others in need. God has given us this wonderful place in His kingdom filled with authority and power to take hold of circumstances supernaturally and see Him change destinies. Let's take up the mantle of the early church and live out the call of God for His people in our own generation.

PRAYER

Father, teach me to believe beyond what is safe for me. Teach me to stretch out for You and Your kingdom, believing that You can still do today what You did for Peter in his day. Amen.

Notes

Days 1–30: Preparing Yourself for Abundant Life

1. James A. Swanson, *A Dictionary of Biblical Languages with Semantic Domains: Aramaic (Old Testament)* (Bellingham, WA: Logos, 2001), computer software, s.v. Sabar.
2. Andrew Murray, *Humility* (New Kensington, PA: Whitaker, 1982), 23.

Days 31–60: Passing God's Tests So He Can Use You

1. From Passover to Pentecost is fifty-two or fifty-three days. Jesus died at Passover and then lay in the tomb for three days (see John 13:1; Mark 9:31). He was with His disciples for forty days after that before returning to heaven (see Acts 1:3). So the disciples prayed in the upper room for ten days before Pentecost, when the Holy Spirit was poured out.
2. D. Martyn Lloyd-Jones, *Reflections: A Treasury of Daily Readings* (Nashville: Thomas Nelson, 1995), 47.
3. Kent Owen, "Sovereignty—Limitations of God," Biblebro.net, www.biblebro.net/sovereignty-limitations-of-god (accessed September 26, 2018).

Days 61–90: Impacting the World Through Powerful Prayer

1. David Reagan, "Favor of God," Learn the Bible, www.learnthebible.org/favor-of-god.html (accessed October 10, 2018).
2. E. M. Bounds, *Purpose in Prayer* (Ada, MI: Baker, 1920), 41.
3. J. Touchette, "David Livingstone's Burial," mysendoff.com, mysendoff.com/2011/07/david-livingstones-burial (accessed October 10, 2018).
4. Ibid., 8.
5. Andrew Murray, Lettie Cowman, "November 2," *Streams in the Desert: 366 Daily Devotional Readings* (Grand Rapids: Zondervan, 1997), 413.
6. A. B. Simpson in Cowman, "November 2," *Streams in the Desert*, 413.

About the Author

Dan Carroll grew up in Pomona, California. In February 1970, he received Christ as his savior at a Youth for Christ meeting. In 1976 he received a B.A. in religion from the University of La Verne and went on to teach in the Pomona Unified School District for three years. Then in 1979 he received his M.A. in education from the Claremont Graduate University. Dan and his wife, Gale, moved to Idaho, where he taught high-school English and history and coached the basketball team. He also served as an elder at Community Fellowship Church.

In 1982 Dan took a youth-pastor position at Life Bible Fellowship in Upland, California, and served there until 1987. He received an M.A. in Christian Ministry from the International School of Theology in 1987.

In 1987 Pastor Dan began teaching a men's Bible study. For three years the study grew in scope and depth, and the families of the men involved began to come together for fellowship. In 1989 Dan and his family went to the Youth With A Mission training school in Kona, Hawaii. They were introduced to cross-cultural ministry in Penang, Malaysia, where Dan received a vision for the world. After returning to the United States in 1990, he was encouraged by the men of his Bible study and their families to plant a church. This became Water of Life Community Church.

Pastor Dan completed a doctorate of ministry from the King's Seminary in 2004. He continues today as the senior pastor of Water of Life Community Church.

Dan and Gale have been married for thirty-nine years and have two adult children, Shane and Katie, who are both married, and three grandsons.

About Water of Life Community Church

Water of Life Community Church is a non-denominational evangelical charismatic church. This means that we are devoted to studying and obeying the Bible, which is the Word of God, and that we believe in the baptism of the Holy Spirit and the modern-day operation of the gifts proclaimed in the New Testament.

Water of Life was established on Sunday, October 28, 1990, when a group of twenty-one adults and eleven children gathered together to worship at the La Petite childcare building in Rancho Cucamonga, California. It was a fellowship that arose from a men's Bible study, a group of people who grew together, and a body that is now committed together to seek God's plan as a church family.

Many people love God but have become disillusioned with the church. Therefore, a church that offers a personal encounter with Jesus Christ and growth in His Word without the clutter of an overly structured environment has great appeal. Because we want to maintain the integrity and purity of our spiritual purpose, we do not have a rigorous structure with multitudes of committees or membership requirements.

Our desire is to walk by faith and in deep trust of our Lord. Consequently, you will not see us take an offering. Rather, we believe that the giving of tithes and offerings is worship to Jesus Christ and an expression of the relationship between each individual giver and the Lord.

Although Water of Life is a non-denominational church, we consider ourselves a church that is interdependent with the rest of the body of Christ. Our church is governed by our pastors and our elder board. Additionally, our senior pastor is accountable to an outside group of senior pastors from other local churches as well as to an internationally recognized leader from the Foursquare denomination.

Our Core Values

HEALING

Healing is the very starting point of a transformed life. It speaks to maturing people into a closer relationship with Christ, not just to getting better inside. Jesus put a huge value on healing—putting people back together again. Healing of sick, wounded, and broken lives is a high priority to a compassionate and loving God:

> The Spirit of the LORD is upon me, for he has anointed me to bring Good News to the poor. He has sent me to proclaim that captives will be released, that the blind will see, that the oppressed will be set free, and that the time of the LORD's favor has come. (Luke 4:18–19, NLT)

Healing is so important to God that He made it a key part of discipleship, or growing in Jesus. Healing occurred many times in Jesus' ministry, and miracles frequently occurred. But Jesus' healing was not just about making people well physically. Rather, it was to restore them in the kingdom of God, to bring them into a right relationship with God. Ephesians 4:11–13 talks of apostles, prophets, evangelists, pastors, and teachers all having the responsibility "to equip God's people to do his work and build up the church, the body of Christ . . . until we all come to such unity in our faith and knowledge of God's Son that we will be mature in the Lord, measuring up to the full and complete standard of Christ" (4:12–13, NLT). The word "equip," *kartatizo* in Greek, means "to mend, restore and be put back together."

> I will sprinkle clean water on you, and you will be clean. Your filth will be washed away, and you will no longer worship idols. And I will give you a new heart, and I will put a new

> spirit in you. I will take out your stony, stubborn heart and give you a tender, responsive heart. And I will put my Spirit in you so you will follow my decrees and be careful to obey my regulations. (Ezek. 36:25–27, NLT)

The goal in all we do must be transformation—that is where winning begins. God has called us into relationship with one another so that we can be healed and then become instruments of His healing.

> Blessed be the God and Father of our Lord Jesus Christ, the Father of mercies and God of all comfort, who comforts us in all our affliction so that we will be able to comfort those who are in any affliction with the comfort with which we ourselves are comforted by God. (2 Cor. 1:3–4)

God does not call us to store up what He gives us but to pass it on to others. Transformation occurs in our church's small groups as well as in our healing and recovery groups, in which people can find support, care, prayer, and encouragement.

SENDING

Sending is our second core value. We believe it is foundational to all that God wants to do in us.

Everything about us likes to be comfortable, but Jesus told us that the way for us to grow is to be stretched out (*ekteno* in the Greek). We need to get out of our comfort zones.

In Acts 13:1–3 we read that the church in Jerusalem sent Paul and Barnabas out on the first real missionary journey. Their goal was to reproduce the work God had done in them and in other believers by spreading the word of Jesus' love and transforming lives and starting churches. This church-planting model has been followed in various forms ever since. Our desire at Water of Life is to send teams out for short-term exposure on a regular basis and at the same time to train and expose our church to as many cross-cultural types of ministry as possible. This includes those near to us (in our valley) and those far from us (all over the world). In our history we have sent short-term teams to between fifteen and twenty different countries, including Malaysia, Hong Kong, Russia, China, Jamaica, Venezuela, Guatemala, Lebanon, Panama, Kenya, Nicaragua, El Salvador, Cuba, and Honduras. More recently, we have sent teams to Mexico, Cambodia, and Thailand.

Jesus told His disciples in Matthew 28:19, "Go therefore and make disciples of all the nations, baptizing them in the name of the Father and the Son and the Holy Spirit." In Acts 1:4–8 He told them more:

> Gathering them together, He commanded them not to leave Jerusalem, but to wait for what the Father had promised, "Which," He said, "you heard of from Me; for John baptized with water, but you will be baptized with the Holy Spirit not many days from now." So when they had come together, they were asking Him, saying, "Lord, is it at this time You are restoring the kingdom to Israel?" He said to them, "It is not for you to know times or epochs which the Father has fixed by His own authority; but you will receive power when the Holy Spirit has come upon you; and you shall be My witnesses both in Jerusalem, and in all Judea and Samaria, and even to the remotest part of the earth."

Jerusalem and Judea were home to Jesus and the disciples—that is, local. So we likewise do local outreach at our food-and-clothing warehouse, with our mobile medical unit, and with our annual Trunk-or-Treat Halloween-alternative event. The remote parts of the world for Water of Life are Cambodia and Thailand as well as other nations we have reached. This outreach is all based on Holy Spirit empowerment, and we seek to establish long-term relationships in each of these areas. This will result in transformed lives—in us as we go and in others as they receive.

EQUIPPING

> And He gave some as apostles, and some as prophets, and some as evangelists, and some as pastors and teachers, for the equipping of the saints for the work of service, to the building up of the body of Christ. (Eph. 4:11–12)

This core value, like the ones before it, speaks to transforming lives. At Water of Life *winning* is defined as "a transformed life demonstrated by a person being given to God and given to other people." In regard to equipping, as we at Water of Life learn the truth in the Word of God, we receive training along with it as to what we are to do with what we learn. Following God is not just about words—it is an action. A changed person is one who loves God and loves people as well as serves God and serves people.

Equipping at Water of Life means more than just attending church or a Bible study: "The things which you have heard from me in the presence of many witnesses, entrust these to faithful men who will be able to teach others also" (2 Tim. 2:2).

At Water of Life, equipping means teaching and releasing people with the purpose of both mind transformation and heart transformation. Practically speaking, all our small groups will teach and do outreach ministry in which they extend themselves to others. Individuals as well are provided with the opportunity to serve by caring for others—putting their knowledge to work to give life to other people.

CARING

> What use is it, my brethren, if someone says he has faith but has no works? Can that faith save him? If a brother or sister

> is without clothing and in need of daily food, and one of you says to them, "Go in peace, be warmed and be filled," and yet you do not give them what is necessary for their body, what use is that? Even so faith, if it has no works, is dead, being by itself. (James 2:14–17)

We believe that one of Water of Life's main priorities is to care for those in need. The principle is this: we get so we can give. We believe this is a part of God's heart for all people. We need the poor and downtrodden as much as they need us. It is through them that we gain the heart of God and the Holy Spirit is able to soften us and impart the Father's heart to us.

The Bible is emphatic about the church's responsibility to care for those in need: "Whoever has the world's goods, and sees his brother [or sister] in need and closes his heart against him, how does the love of God abide in him?" (1 John 3:17).

In Matthew 25 we read that Jesus expects nothing less from His church, which is why this core value is so important at Water of Life.

This expectation is clearly shown in Scripture:

> Then the King will say to those on His right, "Come, you who are blessed of My Father, inherit the kingdom prepared for you from the foundation of the world. For I was hungry, and you gave Me something to eat; I was thirsty, and you gave Me something to drink; I was a stranger, and you invited Me in; naked, and you clothed Me; I was sick, and you visited Me; I was in prison, and you came to Me." (Matt. 25:34–36)

We want to be counted among the faithful described above as those who fed the hungry, gave drink to the thirsty, invited the stranger in, clothed the naked, cared for the sick, and also visited those in prison. "The King will answer and say to them, 'Truly I say to you, to the extent that you did it to one of these brothers of Mine, even the least of them, you did it to Me" (Matt. 25:40).

RELATIONSHIPS

Lives are transformed through relationships—community and family relationships: "You are citizens along with all of God's holy people. You are members of God's family. . . . We [who believe] are carefully joined together in him, becoming a holy temple for the Lord" (Eph. 2:19, 21, NLT).

Everyone who believes in Jesus is part of His family. He has joined us together, and He tells us that we should get along. He is the One who holds everything together. He holds the world together, He holds marriages together, He holds the church family together, and He holds personal relationships together: "He is before all things, and in Him all things hold together" (Col. 1:17).

First Corinthians is quite clear in telling us that He put all of us together; we are one body, and we are supposed to live as if we are:

> For even as the body is one and yet has many members, and all the members of the body, though they are many, are one body, so also is Christ. For by one Spirit we were all baptized into one body, whether Jews or Greeks, whether slaves or free, and we were all made to drink of one Spirit. (1 Cor. 12:12–13)

The rules of the family of God are clear and simple: we are called to serve one another. This is only possible through our relationship with Jesus. To have a powerful and on-fire relationship with Jesus, we have to get our mind off ourselves and choose to focus on other people. Christ always did this. He built His relationships with many people based on compassion, and He asks us to do the same. In Mark 1:41, as Jesus spoke with a leper, He was "moved with compassion." He stretched out His hand, touched the leper, and healed him. In order for us to be really connected with others at a deep level, we must be compassionate.

The heart of a servant is a heart of compassion. There is power in serving others, and there is also blessing in serving others. As we come together in right relationship with other people, we position ourselves to be blessed by God.

Contact us at:

Water of Life Community Church
7625 East Avenue, Fontana, CA, 92336
Water of Life Administration Office
14418 Miller Avenue, Suite K, Fontana, CA 92336
Phone: 909.463.0103
Fax: 909.463.1436